*What Men Believe*

*By the same author:*

Who Cares?: Christianity and Modern Problems
The Life of Christ (Secondary Certificate Questions series)
The Gospels: A First Commentary
Challenge!

# What Men Believe

## F. G. HEROD

*Former Head of Religious Education Department, Catford School*

Methuen Educational

First published 1968
by Methuen Educational Ltd.
11 New Fetter Lane, London E C4P 4E E
Reprinted 1969, 1970, 1972, 1975 and 1978
First published in a net edition 1975
Revised edition first published 1986
© F. G. Herod 1968 and 1986

*Printed in Great Britain*
*by Fletcher & Son Ltd, Norwich*

ISBN 0 423 51330 3 (net)
ISBN 0 423 51200 5 (non-net)

4.12.86

# Contents

CONTENTS

# Foreword

A survey in the north-east of England on 'Religious Education in Schools' made in the late 1960s (P. R. May and O. R. Johnson) showed that while 96 per cent of the parents who answered questionnaires wished their children to be taught about Christianity, 80 per cent wished them to learn about other major religions as well. In recent years the study of world religions has become an essential part of the R.E. curriculum in schools.

I have found that this interest in what other people believe is also shared by the children themselves, who have today a much closer contact with other races than previous generations have known. In satisfying their curiosity, I believe that we are helping them towards inter-racial friendship, as well as teaching them the different paths that men take in their search for truth.

This book, therefore, is the outcome of many years' experience of teaching world religions in the classroom. It attempts to explain in simple language the elements, good and bad, of the chief religions of the world. Theological complications have been deliberately avoided. The chapters are generally of a length suitable for reading in a single lesson and the questions for discussion may encourage further study. In this connection the school library and the assistance of the history department should be valuable. A comparison of beliefs may be made with the help of the index.

Humanism and Communism, not being religious in the strictest sense, are nonetheless added as Communism, in particular, claims the devotion of so many millions in the world it cannot be omitted today from any study of what men believe.

## FOREWORD

I am indebted to the Revised Standard Version of the Bible, to the *New English Bible*, and to the *Bible of the World* (editor Robert O. Ballou) for many quotations from various scriptures. I am also grateful to Mrs. C. M. Pottinger and Mrs. M. A. Young who read the text and offered many useful suggestions.

# Acknowledgements

Thanks are due to the following for permission to use copyright photographs in the illustrations of this book:
Camera Press Ltd for plates 2, 4, 5, 9, 10, 12, 16, 22, 23 and 25; the Australian News and Information Bureau for plate 1; the Government of India Tourist Office for plates 3 and 6; the Thailand Information Bureau for plate 7; the Victoria and Albert Museum for plate 8; the Japanese Embassy Library for plates 13 and 14; the Israel Government Tourist Office for plates 17 and 18; the *Citizen and Gloucester Journal* for plate 20; the Turkish Information Bureau for plate 24; the Radio Times Hulton Picture Library for plate 26; Popperfoto for plates 11, 15 and 21; Barnaby's Picture Library for plate 19; Lion Publishing for the maps of *The World's Religions* and *The Buddhist Lands*.

*Approximate present-day
distribution of the world's religions.*

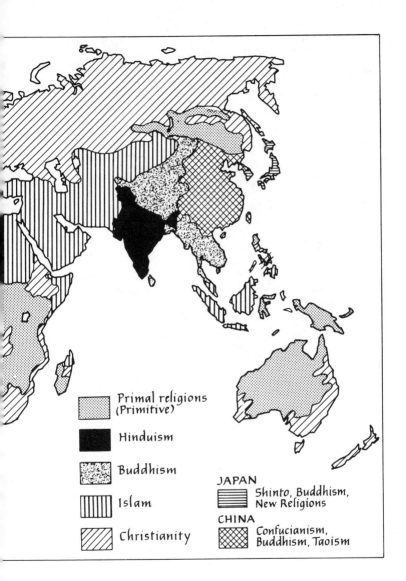

Primal religions (Primitive)

Hinduism

Buddhism

Islam

Christianity

JAPAN
Shinto, Buddhism, New Religions

CHINA
Confucianism, Buddhism, Taoism

## Principal Faiths of Mankind

| Faith | Date of origin | Country of origin | Founder | Writings | Followers* |
|---|---|---|---|---|---|
| HINDUISM | c. 13th century B.C. | India | — | Vedas, Upanishads, etc. | 570 million |
| BUDDHISM | 6th century B.C. | India | Gautama | Various scriptures | 275 million |
| CONFUCIANISM | 6th century B.C. | China | Confucius | Chinese classics | 500 million |
| TAOISM | ? | China | Lao-tze | Tao-te-ching | |
| SHINTO | | Japan | — | Shinto chronicles | 100 million |
| JUDAISM | 20th century B.C. | Palestine | Abraham | Torah and Talmud | 13½ million |
| CHRISTIANITY | 1st century A.D. | Palestine | Jesus | The Bible | 1,200 million |
| ISLAM | 7th century A.D. | Arabia | Muhammad | The Koran | 900 million |
| SIKHS | 16th century A.D. | India | Nanak | Adi Granth | 7 million |
| JAINS | 5th century B.C. | India | ? Mahavira | Jain scriptures | 1½ million |
| PARSEES | 6th century B.C. | Persia | Zoroaster | Avesta | 110,000 |
| COMMUNISM | 19th century A.D. | Germany | Marx | Das Kapital, etc. | 1,350 million |

* The figures in this column should be taken only as a rough estimate of size and influence. Exact numbers are unobtainable. In Communism, for example, the figure is based on the population of the countries under Communist rule.

# Primitive Religion

## 1. The unprivileged

How many of the world's great religions can you name? Most people know two or three and may be able to name the religious leaders who founded them. Not all of them have founders, but they all have sacred writings or scriptures which are deeply respected by their followers. It is these sacred books, carefully preserved down the centuries, which have helped to make them the greatest historic religions of mankind.

Yet in many parts of the world there are religions that have neither founders nor scriptures because they are practised by people who can neither read nor write. We sometimes refer to them, for convenience, as the primitive people of the world, but it should be remembered that over thousands of years they too have advanced in their own way, so that their religion today is not in its earliest form. In every continent except Europe, and in other remote places of the world, such as the northern Tundras and the Pacific Islands, these large uncivilised communities are to be found.

What kind of religion have they? Customs differ widely from one community to another, and some, as, for example, the Zulus and the North American Indians, are more advanced than others. But despite the differences in their way of life, there are certain beliefs, common to all primitive peoples, which help us to understand their behaviour.

### Mana

If you take a walk through the countryside you may come across a high-voltage cable supported by a huge pylon, or a field that is fenced with electrified wiring to prevent cattle straying. In both cases you will be wise to keep your distance because you know that within these things there is an invisible power that can hurt or even kill you.

If, however, you were a member of a primitive tribe you would live in continual fear of an invisible power in many objects around you. We call this imagined power or force by a Melanesian word, *mana*. Belief in *mana* is common to primitive people and affects considerably the way in which they live. Any object which appears to behave in a mysterious fashion, a person, an animal, a tree, a river or even a man-made weapon, may be felt to have this power within it. Such objects are dangerous and must be treated with respect. Anything that is particularly dangerous becomes 'taboo', a word meaning something to be kept away from or something not to be done.

Like electricity, too, this power can be used for the benefit of the tribe. But usually only certain people can control it. In the native village it will be the medicine-man or witch-doctor and possibly the chief, and they will be treated with respect for *mana* flows through them also. The medicine-man, with a certain ritual, will help one man to overcome the ill effects of *mana*, or render another immune from its power, or give to a third the *mana* necessary to accomplish some very difficult task. For this purpose an amulet may be worn, a stone hung round the neck or a bunch of leaves in a hunter's belt. The charm or fetich is a common sight in village huts, on the edge of the jungle, or in any dark or dangerous place. It will at least ward off danger if it does not bring good luck.

We describe *mana* as a primitive belief, yet its influence is by no means dead in our highly civilised world. Many people are superstitious, and charms and taboos play quite a serious part in their lives. It seems that if we cannot believe in the benevolent care of God, we must, like primitive people, look for magic in lesser things.

For *mana* can be thought of as a branch of magic. Another form of magic, which reminds us of witches, is sympathetic magic. This depends on a belief that physical things can act

2

upon one another without actual contact. You make, for example, a wax image of your enemy and stick pins in it, or you destroy a lock of hair, finger-nail clippings, or a piece of clothing belonging to him and he is sure to suffer. The North American Indian draws an outline of his enemy in the dust and jabs it with a pointed stick; the Australian bushman points to his enemy with a special stick on which a curse has been laid. The worker of black magic acts secretly, often at night, and always with the purpose of harming someone. When unexplained tragedy or misfortune falls upon the village, black magic is at once suspected. The medicine-man calls the trembling villagers together and after performing some weird ritual will name the person responsible. An innocent person will sometimes suffer torture and death as a consequence.

In West Africa a special form of magic called *ju-ju* is practised in which spells are cast on people who are disliked. Responsible government officials who have lived out there have testified that this magic does in fact work, and some of them have suffered seriously from its themselves.

Whereas black magic harms, white magic protects. This is the special business of the medicine-man. He is probably a capable and intelligent person with a remarkably wide range of primitive lore. It may include meteorology, primitive surgery, massage, bleeding, childbirth, and the healing powers of plants. He may have psychic powers and be, as well, a keen judge of character. He is expected by potions and formulae to heal diseases, promote successful love-making and marriage, produce rain, guarantee fruitful crops, ensure good hunting and victory in inter-tribal warfare. He is judged by his ability to do these things, and by one means or another he generally has the knowledge or the cunning to satisfy his customers!

## Animism

Imagine a hunter stalking his quarry. As he raises his weapon

3

we notice dangling from one of his fingers a solitary tooth. What possible use could this be to him? Yet he would rather stay at home than leave it behind him on his hunting expeditions, for he believes that within it resides the spirit of a dead friend from whose body he has taken it. His friend was a fine hunter and his tooth is bound to ensure success.

This belief is an advance on *mana*. Belief in a magic force is instinctive; belief in spirits is the result of reasoning. The hunter looks on the body of his friend and realises that his spirit no longer inhabits it in the usual way. He himself has a strange experience too. In sleep he seems to leave his body and wander about the countryside. In this way he interprets dreaming. So he reasons from body to spirit and it is only a natural extension of the idea to believe that almost every object around him has a spirit of its own, animals, rivers, trees, weapons, and tools.

Akin to this belief in spirits that we call animism is the interesting custom found among Australian bushmen and North American Indians of a tribal totem. The Indians, for example, carve a pole into the shape of the animal or plant which is the representative of the tribe. The totem is sacred and the totem animal is never killed and eaten except on ceremonial occasions, when it is then believed that the animal's special qualities are eaten with its flesh. So we have buffalo men, lion men, crocodile men with the totem often tattooed on their bodies. Indians believe that they are the sons of the totem, which may be traced back through their ancestors to the origin of the tribe.

*Polytheism*

It is sometimes difficult in practice to distinguish between *mana* and animism. But polytheism, which is a considerable step forward, is easily recognisable. It is the worship of many gods and is found not only among uncivilised people, but in other parts of the world.

The nature spirits have now become nature gods to be

worshipped, appeased, and served. Notice the bridge between *mana* and a personal god in the custom of the Omaha Indians, for example, who pray to Wakonda, whose name means 'the power that moves'.

Nature gods control the sky and the weather, the earth and the crops, the rivers and the sea. There are special gods in remote places, on high mountains and in the depths of the jungle. The earth gods are often the gods of the dead. But there is usually one god who is thought of as presiding over all the rest. He is the high god who created all things, even the other gods. He dwells in the remote heavens. He laid down the laws by which men should live and he will judge men at the end of life. The belief in a possible happy existence beyond death is general, a heaven suited to the needs of the community: the Indians' Happy Hunting Ground and the Eskimos' ideal country where the sun never sets.

Side by side with the worship of the gods we find the belief that the spirits of the dead are very active. In some cases their interest and activity are welcomed. Zulus, for instance, believe that the spirits of their ancestors fight alongside them on the battlefield. Some Polynesian tribes have special houses in which they keep objects representing their ancestors. Africans are very concerned about the spirits of the dead, consulting them by magical means when important family matters have to be settled. But in Africa the spirits of the dead are often feared. Drums are beaten at funerals to scare them away. Offerings of presents including food are placed on their graves to please them so that they will not return in anger and harm the living.

When we read about the daily life of many of these backward people, we are impressed by the unnecessary sufferings they endure. They fear natural events because they do not understand them; they die from diseases that could easily be cured; and they suffer from laws and customs that are harsh and unjust. Despite the advance of civilisation there are still about one hundred million of such people in the world today.

5

# Points for discussion

1 'Many people are superstitious, and charms and taboos play quite a serious part in their lives.' How many superstitions can you name? Do you think it is harmful to be superstitious? If so, what can be done about it?

2 Today there is a growing interest in astrology. Do you consider there is truth in it or is it just part of our heritage of superstition?

3 It is sometimes asserted that primitive peoples are most wisely left to their own way of life. What is your view?

# Hinduism

## 2. The religion of the Noble Ones

Hinduism is the main religion of India. Though it is many thousands of years old, it still wields a powerful influence over a Hindu population ten times as great as that of the British Isles. To the people of the West it is is full of mystery. Subjects such as yoga, caste, and reincarnation puzzle and fascinate us, and stories of strange customs, of mystics who can perform remarkable feats of physical endurance and who seem to live in a constant state of trance, fill us with curiosity.

What, then, is Hinduism? The answer is far from simple because, unlike other great religions, Hinduism has no founder who proclaimed the faith nor even a date in time when it can be said to have begun. Through countless centuries it has been a very tolerant religion, absorbing many different beliefs about the salvation of man. Thus we find in Hinduism today the greatest wisdom and the most primitive superstition existing side by side, and if we should ask a number of Hindus what they believe about a personal god or a future life, we should be likely to get a number of contradictory answers.

Possibly the easiest way of understanding this complicated religion is to go back as far as we can in its history and see how it has gradually developed.

### The invasion of the Noble Ones

In recent years, archaeologists, working in northern India, have unearthed the remains of a peaceful and well-organized civilisation which existed there 4,500 years ago. The people of this civilisation were known as Dravidians. They were short and squat in build and had dark curly hair. The relics of two of their great cities, Harappa and Mohenjodara, have been uncovered, revealing the remains of palaces, fine houses with courtyards, granaries and baths. The streets were designed in square formation and a sanitation system was discovered more effective than anything India produced afterwards until the nineteenth century. They also devised methods of irrigating their land. It seems that certain rivers were considered sacred and used for ritual bathing. Clay figures and inscriptions on stone suggest that some Dravidian gods were forerunners of later Hindu deities.

Life for these people, however, was not destined to remain peaceful. About the time that Moses was leading the Israelites out of Egypt, another great race was also on the move. This was the Indo-European or Aryan race, which lived in the south-east of Europe somewhere near the Caspian Sea. For reasons unknown to us the Aryans split up into three main sections, one moving west over Europe, another towards the Persian Gulf, and a third into India. They peopled Europe and conquered northern India, and hence we find an interesting resemblance between the Latin and Greek languages, on the one hand, and the ancient Hindu language, Sanskrit, on the other.

The word 'Aryan' means 'noble' or 'distinguished', and these invaders were proud of their height, their strength, and their light skins. In character they were much like the Norsemen who invaded Britain: hard-riding, hard-drinking, hunting, fighting, and quarrelling. They despised the Dravidians, destroying their cities and driving them into the southern part of the peninsula. Contemptuously they referred to them as *dasus*, a word which later they used to mean 'slaves'.

## The religion of the invaders

The Aryans, like the Dravidians, were nature worshippers. They had many gods. Among them were Agni, the fire god, who acted as messenger between gods and men, Vishnu, a minor god, symbolizing the sun, Indra, the storm god and a warrior, sometimes depicted as very drunk and jovial, and in contrast, Varuna, a holy and majestic god demanding high moral standards from his worshippers.

The warrior Aryans worshipped noisily round an altar in the open air. The people sang hymns and the priests chanted incantations and drank large quantities of an intoxicating liquor called *soma*. This *soma* is important because it produced a trance-like ecstasy in which the worshippers felt that they ascended into the heavens. 'We drank *soma* and became immortal,' they declared. So in a primitive way it achieved what yoga was later to produce: an out-of-this-world state of mind – a popular ideal of Hinduism.

About this time another feature of Hinduism was beginning to show itself: the veneration of the cow. In the struggle for existence the rearing of cattle was important. The cow had many uses: the pulling of ploughs and carts and the producing of milk and dung cake. This economic valuation of the cow may well have developed into a religious veneration so that the cow became a sacred animal – so sacred, in fact, that for centuries the penalty for killing one has been death.

As time passed, conquerors and conquered had more to do with each other. The influence of the Dravidian religion on the invaders, for instance, resulted in over thirty gods being worshipped in those early days. Gradually some, like Vishnu, became increasingly important, while others, like Varuna, disappeared.

*The Hindu Scriptures*

Like the Christian Bible the Hindu Scriptures evolved over many centuries. The earliest fragments date back probably to before 1500 B.C., while the later passages were completed about A.D. 200. Though they were enormous in quantity, they were committed to memory by the brahmins, or priests, who wished to keep them jealously to themselves. Eventually, however, they appeared in written form and are widely known and loved throughout India today.

Here, briefly, are their main divisions in the order of their appearance:

*The Vedas* These are the most ancient and important of all the Hindu Scriptures. They consist of four main books of hymns and prayers to the gods, the oldest of which is called the *Rig Veda*. The earliest hymns show a cheerful confidence in the gods; the later ones express some doubt about the meaning of life and the cause of creation. The Vedas are beautifully composed and long passages are learned and quoted by pious Hindus today.

*The Brahmanas* These consist of instructions to the priests on the complicated ritual necessary when sacrificing to the gods. If we realize the power ascribed to the priests – for example, that the sun would not rise unless a priest made sacrifice – we can understand how important these instructions were considered to be.

*The Upanishads* These scriptures are a very important development in Hinduism. They offer almost a new religion in which the priests are no longer necessary; the many gods of Hinduism fade into insignificance and are replaced by one eternal spirit or cause which the seeker can find within himself by earnest meditation.

*The Epic Poems* These are magnificent stories of hero-gods who became men. In one of them, the Ramayana, the story is told of the ideal King, Rama, and his wife, Sita. Rama, as the result of an intrigue, loses his throne and his wife is abducted by a demon, Ravana, and taken to Sri Lanka. Assisted by the monkey god, Hanuman, who builds a monkey bridge from India to Sri Lanka, Rama is able to rescue his wife and on returning home is restored to his Kingdom. Rama is, in fact, an incarnation (avatar) of the god Vishnu. His help is often prayed for at the beginning of any undertaking and he is thanked at its successful conclusion. Sita, too, is regarded as an example of the perfect wife, courteous, pious and loyal to her husband.

The Mahabarata is a story about war, a struggle for power

between two sets of cousins. The highlight of this long poem (90,000 couplets) is found in the sixth book, the Bhagavad-Gita, usually called the Gita or the Song of the Lord.

One of the cousins, Arjuna, is about to do battle against his own kith and kin but though he is a good general he hesitates because he hates war and especially war against his own people. The Gita consists of a dialogue between him and his charioteer, Krishna, who is again the god Vishnu in human form. Krishna's arguments persuade him to fight: he must carry out his duties as a member of the warrior caste and realise that the death of the body is not important because the soul does not die with it. In this life one must do one's duty without hope of reward, work hard, seek knowledge and learn to control one's mind through meditation. Devotion (bhakti) to Krishna will ensure salvation for any man, whatever his caste may be.

This 'Gospel of Krishna' is read and pondered over more than any other Hindu scripture.

## Popular religion today

The vast majority of Indians have inherited their ancestors' love of many gods. In fact, the number of gods now worshipped in India is so great that it is impossible to count them. In every village there are shrines in the home and by the wayside, and gods and godlings, good and evil spirits are the daily concern of the Hindu villagers. But towering above these local deities are the gods of all India known to everyone. They differ considerably in character.

Brahma, the creator, is not generally worshipped, as his work, at least for the present, is considered to be finished. On the other hand, Shiva, the god of destruction, is widely revered. He is portrayed as having four arms and dancing vigorously to show the life-force he controls. He destroys in order to make way for the new. His emblem is a fertility stone (ligna) and worshippers, by offering gifts to him, hope to escape his cruelty. In southern India, however, he is looked upon as a kindly disposed god. His followers, as a sign of devotion, may paint on their foreheads three horizontal lines. This is done with lime and vermilion paint. They also wear rosaries round their necks.

Kali, his female partner, also has two very different aspects. On the one hand she demands blood sacrifices, her forehead bedecked with human skulls and her skirt with severed hands and the ground about her bespattered with blood. On the other hand, she is, for women, the divine mother to whom they should pray for the gift of children.

In complete contrast we have the kindly god Vishnu from whom you will remember sprung the two great heroes, Rama and Krishna. The followers of Vishnu paint on their foreheads three vertical lines.

The homes of the Hindu gods are the great temples scattered over the countryside. Beautiful and majestic in outward appearance, they are often disappointing within. That is possibly because we imagine that a temple is a kind of church where we should find quietness, reverence, and peace. Temples, however, are not churches; they are the palaces of the gods whose huge and curious images gaze down upon devoted worshippers. The priests are their servants and take care of them, treating them as magnificent princes. They are wakened, washed, clothed, fed, amused, taken for rides, and generally kept in apparent good humour, to ensure that they will always listen favourably to the prayers offered to them.

At a certain time each day, the priests announce the offering of sacrifices and prayers by blowing conch shells, and worshippers with their gifts move slowly round the shrine. A passage from the Vedas may also be read by one of the priests. But regular worshippers are few as visits to temples are usually reserved for special occasions. The largest temples with their pyramid shaped towers, courtyards and pools are found in southern India, which escaped the devastations of the Moghul invasions in the north.

In October, the festival of Dasara lasts for ten days. It is held in honour of the goddess Kali and recalls her help in the overthrow of the demon King Ravana. There are processions, dancing and the giving of presents. Huge effigies of Ravana and his followers are packed with crackers and exploded by fiery darts.

In November, the New Year festival Diwali is held. It is a festival of lights and on the night of the new moon people parade the streets carrying small lamps. New clothes are worn and there is much feasting, dancing and present giving. This festival also is in honour of the goddess Kali but more especially the goddess Lakshmi. She is the goddess of good fortune who bestows wealth and prosperity, and is said to visit every house in which a light can be seen on that night. Her help is often sought by businessmen.

In addition very many festivals are held in honour of local gods and other all-India gods such as Shiva. The temples also have their annual festivals when their great images are taken out in procession on decorated carts, sometimes accompanied by elephants and bathed in near-by rivers. Pilgrimages to holy places often end in a round of festivities. These occasions help to maintain and strengthen family and community ties.

Worship (puja) in the home, however, is general. If a room is not set aside, at least a corner is reserved for the favourite family deity. Here an image, or in poor households pictures of the god are treated with great reverence. The devotional exercises are similar to those in temples. The image is cooled with water, dressed and offered food. Flowers and coloured powder are used for ornamentation; lamps are lit and verses (mantras) from the Vedas are recited. This is followed by meditation. The women of the household usually look after the shrine, and may, in fact, have images of their own as, for example, the young Krishna. If the family is a very busy one, at least one member representing it will perform the ceremonies which take place three times daily, early morning, noon, and in the evening.

Among the higher classes (castes) a man's part in the daily devotions is most important. If near a river, he bathes just before dawn. Then sitting bare to the waist, cross-legged on the ground he utters the sacred word OM with a long drawn-out humming sound and repeats the name of the god he is worshipping. He sips water, sprinkles it on the ground around him and then touches his body in six places to indicate that god is within him. He binds up his loose hair on to the crown of his head and recites the gayatri: 'Let us meditate on the most excellent light of the Creator; may he guide our intellect'. This sacred mantra is repeated many times a day. Finally, with his face towards the rising sun, his eyes focused on the tip of his nose and his breathing carefully controlled he meditates, seeking complete union with his god. In a shortened form he repeats this ritual at noon and in the evening.

In Hinduism there is no special day in the week set aside for religious observances. There are, however, many festivals during the year, both local and national in which everyone normally takes part.

In February there is the spring Festival, Holi. Processions, bonfires and dancing take place. Stories about Krishna and his love for Radha are recounted and in a happy mood men, specially dressed for the occasion, paint their faces, squirt dye over their friends, and may pour buckets of it over them – if they can be cornered! Everyone is out for enjoyment; it is possibly the most popular of the annual festivals.

# Hinduism

## 3. The endless cycle of life and death

The worship of many gods, polytheism, as we find it in India today has little practical interest for us, but the third section of the Hindu Scriptures, the Upanishads, offers us a new theory about life which is worth careful study.

### Reincarnation

Most religions teach survival after death, but reincarnation teaches survival in an unusual form. Though our earthly bodies decay, the life-force within us is eternal. The spirit or personality of a man lives on, but takes upon itself another body on earth. This process continues endlessly. According to this view we have all lived on earth hundreds of times before our present existence and shall continue to return for many hundreds of lives to come. Our physical body is therefore like a suit of clothes, to be discarded for a new one when it is worn out.

Many arguments have been advanced in favour of this theory. For example, if on rebirth we bring something with us from our past lives, this might account for the mysterious fact of genius. How is it that from an ordinary family one child sometimes emerges with the most extraordinary talent and becomes world-famous? According to the theory of reincarnation this could simply be the re-entry of an exceptional personality into the world in a new body. Again, a queer sensation many people have is to recognize some new experience through which they are passing. 'I have been here before,' they exclaim, yet they know full well that in this life, at least, they can never have been there before. Reincarnation has an obvious explanation for this mysterious problem. The curious experience of love at first sight has been explained as the reunion of kindred souls from a past existence. Whether such arguments as these impress us or not, the fact remains that reincarnation is a theory of life accepted without question by Hinduism and also by a later religion, Buddhism.

This belief is coupled with what we may feel is a strange attitude to our earthly existence: that life in this world has little meaning or purpose. It is argued that all desire and ambition produce suffering; even the desire to be born and to live is bad, for it is the beginning of pain and sorrow. Many Hindus believe also that the world is unreal (maya), that we only imagine it to exist, and that, in effect, it is simply a very bad dream. If we add to this depressing view the belief that we can be reborn in the form of a lower animal, a snake or a worm, for instance, the prospect of endless existences on earth is a very gloomy one indeed. Consequently, the real aim of the Hindu who has considered these things is to break the chain of unending births and deaths and find eternal release from earthly life. This he can do if he concentrates his whole thought on *Brahman*.

## Brahman

First we should note that this word has nothing to do with Brahma, the creator god. Brahman is the eternal spirit of the universe. Belief in this eternal spirit excludes any serious thought of other gods. If they exist, they must be created by *Brahman*, for *Brahman*, as in the following quotation from the Upanishads, is the essence of everything.

> 'Thou art man, thou art woman. Thou art the dark blue bee and the green parrot with red eye. . . . Thou art the seasons and the seas. Thou dost abide with all pervadingness wherefrom all things are born.'

How, then, are we related to *Brahman*? Hinduism teaches that in one sense we are not separate persons at all. Our bodies are separate, it is true, but our bodies are not our real selves. All the little selves that make up the human race are really linked together and are one self, and all are part of *Brahman*. For each of us, the discovering of the real self, *atman*, which lives majestically within us, controlling our bodies, thoughts, and emotions, is the beginning of true knowledge.

The Hindu who sees nothing in life but sorrow and whose aim is eternal dreamless sleep must therefore turn within himself in deep contemplation. He must release for all time his soul or self from the imprisonment of the body. Suicide, of course, is no way out, for he would return to this world in another physical form. He is taught that the only way is by a strict form of self-discipline known as yoga.

## Yoga

For many Western people this word represents the mysterious and little known powers of the East. They have heard of yogi – those who practise yoga – performing remarkable feats of endurance without suffering: walking or lying upon metal spikes, eating glass with apparent relish, and remaining alive after being buried for long periods. We can partly understand this when we remember that yoga is akin to self-hypnotism, and hypnotism has a remarkable power over the human body. In a trance a person's body behaves as it is ordered to by the hypnotist. It can be made to believe, for example, that a very hot object applied to the skin is cold, and it does not feel the pain which in a waking state it would find intolerable. Yogi practise mental and bodily subjection for years and therefore the self control they acquire is exceptional.

The true purpose of yogi is not to perform feats of endurance for their own sake but to achieve release from earthly life (Moksha) and union with Brahman. For this purpose a Hindu is encouraged to leave home and seek the solitude of the jungle. There, by strict rules of diet, posture, breathing, and intense concentration, he turns his mind inwards in search of the Supreme Being.

17

Here are the instructions to yogi as given in the Hindu Scriptures:

> 'The yogi planteth his own seat firmly upon a spot that is undefiled, neither too high nor too low, and sitteth upon the sacred grass which is called *kusha*, covered with a skin and a cloth. There he, whose business is the restraining of his passions, should sit with his mind fixed on one object alone, keeping his head, his neck and body steady without motion, his eyes fixed on the point of his nose, looking at no other place around.'

Though only a small minority of Indians practise this rigorous form of yoga, it makes a strong appeal to Indian people. The genuine yogi is greatly venerated as a holy man and to kiss his feet is a privilege. Some of these holy men are found in charge of temples; others teach with a small group of disciples about them; others travel from one village to another where they are often considered to have the power to banish evil spirits. But they spend much of their lives in solitude and silence, and though we may not understand and agree with their view of life, they have something to teach a noisy, over-busy civilisation about the value of meditation and the hidden powers of the mind.

A milder form of yoga is practised by many Hindus who live a normal life in society. There is, for example, the discipline of prayer and meditation, already described, carried out three or more times a day. It is a common practice to invoke the aid of one's god in order to know and understand *Brahman*, as in the following meditation:

> 'I am the Lord, in no-wise different from him, the *Brahman*. I suffer from no pains or ills. I am existence and knowledge and bliss, ever free. O Lord of the world, all intelligence, and greatest God, O Vishnu, as I awake early in the morning I shall fulfil all the duties of my daily life.'

Then there is the very popular worship of Krishna. In return for a discipline of worship and service, Krishna (sometimes called Hare) promises his followers eternal union with himself.

The Hindu takes his religion very seriously. Through his daily meditation he is able to acquire an inward peace and self-assurance with which to face the hardships of life, which in India are many. Later in life he may make a pilgrimage to one of India's holy places. The most important of these is Benares on the banks of the Ganges. The river is considered sacred and thousands of pilgrims bathe in it each year. Benares is also a good place in which to die, for it is said that those who do so go straight to heaven.

## Caste

In the Hindu Scriptures there is a description of how caste first came from Brahma, the creator: from his mouth came the priests, *Brahmins*, from his breast the warriors, *Kshatriyas*, from his thighs the merchants and husbandmen, *Voisyas*, and from his feet the servants, *Sudras*. This is the famous fourfold order of Hinduism into which in the beginning the population of Hindu India was said to be divided – all but the millions known as outcastes, or Untouchables.

The caste system certainly dates from antiquity, but it is doubtful whether at any time there were only four castes. The invading Aryans treated the Dravidians as a lower order of humanity, and at the same time the brahmins were struggling with the rulers and military classes to win for themselves a position of superiority in the social order. They won their battle and became the supreme caste, though few of them nowadays are priests. Gradually in this way perhaps the rigid caste system arose. Today there are many thousands of sub-castes, but the general social levels are clearly defined: high-caste, low-caste, and outcaste.

The power of caste is tremendous. Children are born into the caste of their parents and cannot change it. Marriage between castes rarely takes place. One caste does not eat with another and physical contact with a lower caste is forbidden.

Almost every aspect of life comes within its influence: how people dress, the food they eat, and the work they do.

Caste is directly related to reincarnation, since one's behaviour in this life will decide in what form one returns in the next. This could mean a higher or a lower caste, or as an animal, an insect, or even as a woman. This is known as the law of *Karma*, expressed elsewhere as, 'Whatsoever a man soweth that shall he also reap.'

The worst feature of the caste system has been the existence in India of forty million pariahs or outcastes. Their plight through history has been a terrible one. Despised by the rest of their fellow-men as Untouchables, they have been communal slaves, owned by the village to which they happened to be attached. They have always been required to do the work that the other villagers would not touch, such as attending to the primitive sanitation of the community, the removal and disposal of dead beasts, and the curing of hides. At all times they have had to keep their distance from the other villagers and their lot has been much like that of the leper in medieval Europe. It was their unhappy fate that inspired much of Gandhi's social work. 'If I have to be reborn,' he declared, 'I would wish to be born an Untouchable, so that I might share their sorrows, their sufferings and the affronts levelled at them, in order that I might endeavour to free myself and them from their miserable condition.'

A further point about caste is important. You may remember how difficult it seemed to define Hinduism. As we trace its growth we discover no distinguishing feature of belief or worship that all Hindus share. But there is one bond that unites them: the caste system. All Hindus belong to this system whatever they believe. It is impossible for a stranger to become a Hindu. Occasionally it has happened that whole tribes have become Hindu, but only where they have been prepared to form an entirely new caste. Hinduism has never been a missionary religion; it began in India and remains there. Nevertheless, the influence of Hinduism is seen in certain movements that spread from India to the west. Here are two of the most important.

Sri Ramakrishna (1836–86) was a Brahmin who early in life began to have ecstatic experiences. As a young man he became chief priest in a temple to Kali in Calcutta. There followed visions of Sita, Rama, Krishna, Muhammad and Christ. Ramakrishna then left the temple and went into solitude for twelve years tended only by his wife. This experience completely changed his beliefs. Henceforth he taught that all religions contained important truths; they were in fact different paths that led to God. He therefore mingled freely with people of other faiths adopting their dress, their food, their customs and their worship. For a Hindu of the highest caste to behave in this way was revolutionary but his piety and sincerity impressed people deeply and his influence while he lived was considerable, especially in Calcutta. After his death a mission was established in his name which spread into Europe and America where his teaching and the educational and charitable work which result from it continue today.

Another movement based on Hinduism but including Buddhist and Christian ideas is theosophy. Its founders were a Russian, Mme. Helena Blavatski, and an American, Colonel Odcott. Its basic teaching is Hindu and that is why, though it was founded in New York in 1875, its centre was transferred to India in 1878. Mme. Blavatski claimed to have received wisdom from teachers in northern India who interpreted for her secret knowledge from the Hindu Scriptures. Theosophy stresses the ideas of pantheism (god in everything), Karma and reincarnation and maintains that from time to time special teachers are sent into this world to instruct mankind in the divine wisdom. Branches of the Theosophical Society are to be found in Europe and America.

# Hinduism

## 4. Hinduism and the New Constitution

In these days no nation can live to itself. For better or worse, modern science is drawing the immense populations of the world into one compact human family. In most countries even the remotest villages are awaking to a new life. Air travel has shattered their centuries of solitude; the radio has brought them fascinating glimpses of a new world; and central governments are busily organizing their education and social life. All this is happening in India today, as in other countries of the East.

In addition to the general disturbance, India, in recent years, has undergone a great political upheaval. In 1947, after a century and a half of British rule, India became self-governing. When the actual transfer of power took place there was a tremendous upsurge of patriotism. India now belonged to the Indians, and with great enthusiasm they set about transforming it into a modern progressive state.

Amongst those who wished to see their country rescued from the poverty, ignorance and caste prejudice that degraded it, one figure stands out supreme, Mahatma (Great Soul) Gandhi.

Gandhi was born in 1869 into the merchant caste. At the age of nineteen he travelled to England to train as a barrister. Immediately he qualified he went to South Africa to see what he could do as a lawyer to help the many thousands of his fellow countrymen who had settled there and were badly treated. After working for them for twenty-one years he returned to India to join in the great struggle for freedom and to champion the millions who suffered under the caste system.

Many British people had felt that the time had come to withdraw from India. In fact, as far back in history as Gladstone the subject of Indian home rule had been mooted. But progress was all too slow and it was Gandhi's long campaign that hastened independence. His method of fighting was by non-co-operation and non-violence. Between 1920 and 1944, he was imprisoned many times. He also fasted, threatening to 'fast unto death' on several occasions in his struggle to help the Untouchables. On 30 January 1948, on his way to prayer, he was murdered by a Hindu fanatic.

His way of life was simple. When he left home he promised his mother that he would never eat meat, take alcohol or smoke. He kept that promise all his life. He dressed like a peasant, weaving his own clothes. He disliked western industrial towns and believed that simple village life was ideal for India.

He was a very devout man. He would not allow any business however important to interfere with his set times each day for prayer and meditation. He drew his beliefs from many religions. He once said, 'I am a Muslim, a Sikh, a Christian and a Jew'. To his followers he gave this rule of life:

'I shall not fear anyone on earth. I shall fear only God. I shall not bear ill-will towards anyone. I shall not submit to injustice from anyone. I shall conquer untruth by truth and in resisting untruth I shall put up with any suffering.'

The results of his great efforts and of those who worked with him were enshrined in a New Constitution for his country. Here is the introduction or Preamble to it. Henceforth the object of government would be to secure for all citizens of India:

> JUSTICE, social, economic and political;
> LIBERTY of thought, expression, belief, faith, and worship;
> EQUALITY of status and opportunity;
> and to promote among them all
> FRATERNITY, assuring the dignity of the individual and the unity of the Nation.

23

It is clearly stated here that liberty of faith and worship would be safeguarded. Thus the Hindu religion would be upheld. But there is one important condition: that men should be free and enjoy equality in the eyes of the law. Now much in Hinduism, as we must have realized, is contrary to these ideals, and accordingly great changes would be necessary. Let us look, for example, at the way India is tackling two of the major problems that arise directly from Hinduism: caste and the status of women.

## The New Constitution and caste

Before India became an independent republic there were serious attempts, chiefly by Christian missions, to improve the life of the outcastes. Finally, Gandhi roused the national conscience on their behalf. He called them *Harijan*, 'the Children of God', and at last with Article 17 of the Constitution we have the declaration:

> 'Untouchability is abolished and its practice in every form is forbidden.'

Henceforth, the term 'outcaste' should have no legal meaning. The Untouchables have become known as 'the Scheduled Castes'. They are being educated, they have the right to vote and their own representatives sit in parliament.

The problem of the Untouchables, however, is only a small part of a much greater issue. According to the Constitution, all caste privilege should disappear. This demands a complete revolution in the life of the Indian people. It aims at equality of status and opportunity for everyone. Whether this ideal can be realised only the future will tell. Every society, however democratic, tolerates privilege of some sort, whether it is based on money, birth, education, or on other considerations. In India, for thousands of years, it has been caste. By Hindu law, for example, a brahmin may commit the most terrible crimes and often escape punishment, but an outcaste, if he so much as spoke unpleasantly of another caste, could be seriously mutilated. Such inequalities should disappear. Furthermore, caste distinctions, which can easily be maintained in the village, survive with difficulty in the towns. How can the bustling crowds working in mills, eating in public restaurants, and travelling on public transport maintain the difficult prohibitions of caste? This has proved almost impossible. Consequently, for years outcastes have been drifting from the country into the towns in the hope of enjoying a fairer share of the life of the community.

The effect of the Constitution on rural India is quite another matter. The whole basis of village life is caste, and without its privileges village life must be entirely reorganised. Caste is so deeply engrained in Indian life, so completely bound up with the day-to-day religious observances, that it will take many years, if not generations, to realise throughout India the aims of the Constitution.

## The New Constitution and women

Under ancient Hindu law a woman has very few rights. She can hold no property of her own and is therefore entirely dependent upon her male relatives. Her function in life is to marry, to have children, and to bring them up. When she is married, her husband takes her to live in his parents' home, and there she must find her place and be content with life among her 'in-laws', who may dominate her life for many years. There are many passages in the Hindu Scriptures about the duties of wives to their husbands, as, for example:

> 'When in the presence of her husband, a woman must not look on one side or the other. She must keep her eyes on her master to be ready to receive his commands. When he speaks, she must be quiet and listen to nothing besides. When he calls her, she must leave anything else and attend to him alone.'

If her husband should die, her life too is looked upon as finished. She is not expected to marry a second time, and often ekes out a lonely and unwanted existence. In fact, when the British first went to India, they found there the terrible practice of a widow being forced by custom to throw herself upon the blazing pyre that consumed her husband's remains. It was believed that a woman doing this would win great merit for herself and her husband. 'A widow who burns herself receives for herself and her husband enjoyment for as many years as there are hairs on the human body.' Child marriage was also a feature of Hindu life, and small girls were frequently married to fully grown men. British rule made the worst excesses illegal, and managed, for the most part, to stamp them out.

We must not assume from all this that a woman's life in India has necessarily been an unhappy one. A Hindu mother often receives the honour and respect of her husband and children, but this has depended in the past on the character of the family rather than on any natural rights she might enjoy. Under ancient Hindu law, the law of Manu, a woman ranks more as the property of her husband than as his equal, and he can, in fact, treat her very much as he likes. Moreover, so much has been said and written about the stupidity and foolishness of womankind that it is not surprising that she has been regarded as an inferior being, whose mental capacities cannot compare with those of her husband.

In modern India, however, this attitude is changing. Long before 1947 Gandhi appealed to the women of India to help him in his great work for reform. Thousands of them responded. They worked with him in his campaigns for the outcastes and for other major reforms. The respect and prominence which they earned contributed to the great advances forecast in the New Constitution. According to its provisions, women are no longer inferior to men. They can inherit and hold property. Thus they may live a life of complete independence if they wish. The highest education is open to them, and, as in other progressive states, many of them are distinguishing themselves in the professions and in politics. In the towns they are slowly achieving equality with men. In rural India, however, ancient laws and customs die very slowly. And India is a vast country of villages. Here we look for tendencies to reform rather than sweeping changes. But gradually with the slow spread of enlightenment the women of India should realize a new and fuller life.

## The future of Hinduism

The pace of reform in India has been much slower than was hoped in 1947. The country, of course, is vast – the size of Western Europe – and the problems immense. Many new laws giving effect to the Constitution are on the statute book but real progress towards justice, liberty and equality requires the will of rulers and people working in harmony.

The blurring of caste divisions in the cities arises, as we have seen, from necessity. But in the 700,000 villages that make up eighty per cent of India's population there is no such necessity. The scheduled castes have gained little from the new Constitution. For the most part their lives continue grim and poverty-stricken, their labour often exploited by rich landowners. For many of their fellow-countrymen they still remain simply Untouchables. The temples into which Gandhi led them and the wells which he encouraged them to use are avoided by caste Hindus. And in village society where widows are still expected to eke out their lives in wretched solitude the Law of Manu prevails.

Another serious problem since independence has been the continuation of communal riots. The pursuit of liberty for belief and worship should have resulted in harmony between the various religions in India but this is far from the case. Religious minorities, such as Muslim, Sikh and Christian, have felt themselves continually in danger.

By far the largest of them consists of 60,000,000 Muslims. Riots directed against them have been frequent. Very many thousands have been murdered and many more have lost their homes and businesses. Even in the crowded streets of busy towns Muslims have been at risk. They have sought

27

protection from the government in vain. They have been treated as second class citizens, with even their language, Urdu, threatened with official extinction. They maintain that there are too many high caste Hindus in power who have turned a blind eye to their dreadful sufferings.

In matters of religion then little progress seems to have been made. But Gandhi is not forgotten: his statues are everywhere and he is greatly revered and believed by many to have been a modern avatar. There is still hope by many people of goodwill in India that his ideals may be revived and a more just and peaceful way of life may gradually emerge.

# From the Hindu Scriptures

He is the one god, hidden in all beings, all-pervading, the self within all beings, watching over all words, dwelling in all beings. The wise who perceive him within their self, to them belongs eternal happiness.

(Upanishads)

As a man, casting off worn-out garments, taketh new ones, so the dweller in the body, casting off worn-out bodies, entereth into others that are new.

(*Gita*)

This human body entombs a self which is nothing if not a worker. It is the works of this self in a prior existence which determine the nature of its organism in the next, as well as the character of the diseases, whether physical or mental, which it is to fall prey to.

(Puranas)

Forget all the worldly knowledge that thou hast acquired and become as ignorant as a child and then wilt thou get the divine wisdom.

(*Sri Ramakrishna*)

The man who is full of faith obtaineth wisdom, and he also who hath mastery over his senses and, having obtained wisdom, he goeth swiftly to the supreme peace.

(*Gita*)

He who beareth no ill-will to any being, friendly and compassionate, without attachment and egoism, balanced in

29

pleasure and pain, and forgiving, ever content, with the self controlled, with mind and reason dedicated to me, he, my devotee, is dear to me.

*(Gita)*

Different creeds are but different paths to reach the Almighty. Various are the ways that lead to the house of the Lord. Every religion is nothing but one of such paths that lead to God.

*(Sri Ramakrishna)*

# Points for discussion

1 What evidence is there for and against reincarnation?

2 What is yoga? Has its practice anything to teach us about the power of the human mind?

3 What are the advantages and disadvantages of the caste system in India? How does it compare with the class privileges in other countries?

4 What changes in the Hindu religion are essential under the New Constitution (p 21)?

5 What do you know of the life and teaching of Mahatma Gandhi?

6 Is the way of non-violence the best method for achieving reform?

# Buddhism

## 5. The life and teaching of Buddha

In the sixth century B.C. there lived in a palace on the slopes of the Himalayas the son of an Indian prince. His name was Gautama, later to be known as the Buddha, the Enlightened One. His father adored him, surrounding him with every possible luxury and shielding him from all the unpleasant experiences of life. He was not allowed to see anything painful; the sorrows of ill-health, old age, and death were carefully guarded from him. He had a beautiful young wife and, later, became the father of a fine baby son. Yet despite his father's care, we are told that Gautama often suffered from a vague sense of uneasiness and fear.

One day, unknown to his father, he took a long drive into the neighbouring country. As the road had not been specially cleared for him, he encountered on the way three tragic figures: a sick man, an old man, and a dead man. In each case Gautama asked his driver what the sorry spectacle meant. 'This comes to us all,' was the repeated answer. Deeply affected by his discovery, Gautama had only one thought: how can a man escape the terrible tragedies of life? 'Old age is coming on,' he meditated, 'with its loss of power and health; sickness and death may intervene; death will bring new suffering.'

In India, as we have discovered, wisdom is often associated with men who give up normal living and resort to the jungle and to wandering alone over the countryside. Gautama met such a man and resolved that to solve the mystery of life, which he now urgently wanted to do, he should become 'a holy man' himself. So stealthily one night, leaving his wife and baby asleep, he crept out of the palace and with his servant rode away. At dawn, having reached the limits of his father's domain, he sent back his servant with his horse, his sword, and all his valuables. Later he found a beggar with whom he exchanged clothes. Nothing at all now remained of his former life and he wandered on alone.

He had many adventures. First he lived with two celebrated brahmin teachers and became as famous as they. But Hinduism did not help him. He said that it led 'neither to disgust with the world nor release from passion nor to annihilation nor to peace nor to spiritual knowledge'. So with five friends he turned to yoga. In the jungle he practised fasting and meditation, until one day as a result of starvation he fell down unconscious. When he came to himself again he realised how stupid it was to abuse his body in this way. To the disgust of his friends he sat down to a good meal. They left him and again he wandered on alone.

Some time later he rested under a pipal tree and remained there several days in meditation. He had a remarkable vision of all his previous lives on earth and then quite suddenly he knew the solution to his problem. He called it 'The Middle Way of Deliverance', a path of self-discipline lying between the extremes of palace luxury and the hardships of yoga.

Buddhists regard the spot where Gautama sat as the centre of the world, and a temple stands there today. The pipal or bo-tree lives many hundreds of years, and a cutting from Gautama's tree was planted centuries later in Sri Lanka, where it still grows among the ruins of the old capital.

With his 'Middle Way of Deliverance' Gautama now felt he had the means to break the cycle of life and death and eventually to leave this world for ever. But he chose instead to spend his life teaching his fellow-men the Way of Deliverance. He began at Benares, where his five former friends became his first disciples. For forty-five years, we are told, he travelled India, teaching with remarkable success. When he died his body was cremated, and his ashes, divided into ten parts, were sent to the various provinces where he had lived and taught. Other relics of the Buddha, such as hair and teeth, are said to be preserved in different parts of the world.

## The teaching of Buddha

Our chief information about Buddha's teaching comes from the Buddhist Scriptures. The earliest ones contain a statement of faith, rules for monks, and an extremely difficult handbook of philosophy for monks to study. But they are based on documents written four hundred years after Buddha's death. As a consequence, there have been many arguments as to what exactly Buddha taught. The best we can do is to assume that the early Scriptures give us his original teaching and show how it developed later in different ways.

Buddha, brought up as a Hindu, accepted the ideas of reincarnation and of the final release from earthly existence that Buddhists call nirvana. But he hated the caste system, considered priests unnecessary, and rejected yoga as a way of life.

His teaching was based upon four statements about life known as 'the Four Noble Truths', and eight rules of conduct, 'the Eightfold Path of Deliverance'. Considering Buddha's Hindu background, we shall not be surprised at the following statements he makes about the evil nature of life.

1 *The fact of suffering* All earthly life is full of suffering. Birth, sickness, old age, and death are all accompanied by pain and misery. Throughout life we are continually unhappy, seeking to obtain the things we like and to be rid of the things we dislike. Thus we are always suffering and the sum of life is misery.

2 *The cause of suffering* The root cause of suffering is desire. We desire to live or to die, to live after death, to achieve fame, wealth, or the pleasures of the senses. These selfish desires account for the misery of life.

3 *The end of suffering* The end of all desire, therefore, is the

end of all suffering. As soon as we cease to desire anything at all, even life itself, we cease to suffer.

4 *The escape from suffering* To assist the escape from suffering one must take the Middle Way, the Noble Eightfold Path of self-discipline. This consists briefly of right beliefs, right aims, right speech, right conduct, right employment, right effort, right thinking, and right meditation.

These eight rules divide naturally into three sections. The first two describe the attitude of mind of a Buddhist convert. He must have accepted the Four Noble Truths as the correct view of life and his aim must be nirvana, sacrificing everything else in life to achieve it.

The next three, speech, conduct, and employment, concern his relations with the world around him. He must be careful in conversation, indulging neither in idle gossip nor useless argument. He will be self-controlled, courteous, and considerate. He must keep five rules: not to kill, steal, lie, commit adultery, or take alcohol or drugs. His daily work must be in accordance with his principles: a good Buddhist, for example, could not be a butcher or a wine merchant.

But the most important directions are contained in the last three rules: right effort, right thinking, and right meditation. By them he learns to control the whole of his mind. Statues of Buddha usually show him seated with eyes closed, withdrawn from the world and completely absorbed in the life of the mind. This is the true aim of Buddhism, but the mental exercises required to achieve it are so intense and prolonged that the Buddhist must sacrifice the remainder of his life to them. The life of the mind becomes real only as the physical world recedes. As the Buddhist approaches the state of nirvana the world has less and less meaning for him until finally he leaves it for ever.

*Buddhist moral teaching*

As part of the mental and physical discipline required by the

35

Buddhist way of life, Buddha laid down certain excellent rules of conduct.

Buddhists must not take life. According to Buddhist teaching all life is one and to kill is to sin against oneself. A Buddhist is careful to strain his tea lest he should by accident kill and swallow a stray insect. He will not of course kill animals for food, though he will eat meat that is provided for him, because Buddha insisted that his followers should always accept the food given to them wherever they went.

Buddhists are to be peacemakers. When Hindus, and later Muslims, attacked Buddhism in India there was some resistance, but the majority of Buddhists remained pacifist. In kindness and charity to all men Buddhists have set a fine example to the world. They are required to be patient in suffering and resigned under misfortune.

The physical side of life is looked upon as evil, eventually to be got rid of altogether. The Buddhist must therefore learn to detach 'himself' from his body. If, for example, he has an aching tooth, he regards the tooth as something altogether separate from 'himself'. Consequently, by refusing to allow his thoughts to dwell upon physical pain, he largely destroys its power over him. We can see how this discipline, highly developed, could enable Buddhist monks to burn themselves to death, as they have done in recent years in Saigon, on behalf of what they feel to be a worthy cause.

Other Buddhist laws remind us of the Jewish Ten Commandments. Buddhists may not steal. They may gain wealth but they must acquire it honestly. They must not commit adultery. They must always speak the truth; even exaggeration is lying. They must not drink intoxicants or take drugs since they are unnecessary to health and encourage laziness.

*God, the soul and eternal life*

On some of the most important questions that spring to our minds when we think of religion, Buddha was not very clear. Was he an atheist? We cannot be sure. After he had received his revelation under the pipal tree he declared, 'I am all-wise; I am free from stains; I have no teacher; no one is my equal; in the world of men and gods no being is like me. I am the holy one of the world.' It seems that even if Buddha believed in one god or many, the subject was quite unimportant to personal salvation. To his disciples he said, 'Take the self as your refuge. Look not for refuge to anyone beside yourself.'

There is difficulty also in deciding what Buddha taught about the soul. He used the term 'self' for soul. The self was a mixture of thoughts, sensations, and emotions as unstable as the particles of dust in a sunbeam. At death nothing of them remained. Yet if this is true, how can there be personal reincarnation? When Buddha was asked about this he seems to have brushed aside the question as unimportant.

This brings us to the subject of eternal life. Many Buddhists distinguish between the permanent and temporal parts of the self. They speak of nirvana as an experience in this life and *pari*-nirvana as an experience in the next. Yet they differ as to the meaning of nirvana. It is a state of mind, we are told, lying somewhere between existence and non-existence! But on one point all Buddhists are agreed. It is the most wonderful of all experiences: a state of freedom, joy, and peace that comes when a man's life is empty of all desire and completely free from those things that can never satisfy him.

# Buddhism

## 6. How Buddhism developed

As we have seen, the main object of Buddha's teaching was to show mankind how to escape for ever from the evils of earthly existence. To be alive meant to suffer; the older we grew, the worse suffering became. To be faced then with an endless sequence of reincarnations, to go on suffering in this way to eternity, was something not to be borne. Those who wished therefore to be rid of this burden once and for all would follow the Buddha's teaching, but it would mean nothing less than devoting the remainder of one's life to an iron self-discipline.

### An order of monks

It was accordingly an order of monks which Buddha founded, men who forsook 'the daily round and common task', resorted to the jungle and spent the rest of their days studying and practising the Eightfold Path. Here are some of the earliest rules laid down for the Buddhist monk (Bhikkhu):

(a)  to dress in rags;
(b)  to wear a yellow cloak over his rags;
(c)  to eat only once a day;
(d)  to possess nothing, only that given him in his begging bowl;
(e)  not to handle money;
(f)  to live for part of the year in the forest with only a tree for shelter and to sit on a carpet even when asleep. To lie down was forbidden.

In order to provide clothes for himself, the monk used to

visit the rubbish tips in the neighbouring village. He would select a few rags, sew them together, and dye them yellow. These would be his only protection against the weather in all seasons, since life under any kind of roof was frowned upon.

In order to provide himself with food he had to beg. This required great self-discipline for it was a rule that everything put into the bowl must be eaten, including the dirtiest and most repulsive scraps of food. Buddha himself, brought up to luxury, faced his first bowl of food with a terrible sense of revulsion. Then he began to eat and afterwards the discipline gradually became easier. His disciples followed his example literally. It is recorded, for instance, that one monk ate a leper's thumb that accidentally fell off into his bowl. In begging, a monk must take refusals, insults, even violence, with complete indifference. He must express neither gratitude nor annoyance. He must not raise his eyes to his benefactor, and as he walked, he gazed steadily before him, glancing neither to right nor left.

On one other matter affecting his relations with other people a monk had to be extremely careful: his attitude to women. Having taken the vows of the Buddhist order he completely severed his relations with the opposite sex. He would not even look at a woman if he could avoid it. Gautama himself seemed to have felt that women were not only useless but a positive danger to the success of his work. When women threatened to join his order he despaired and prophesied its destruction. 'Do not look at them, do not speak to them,' he warned his followers. One illustration of how they should behave is given in this way. If your mother falls into the river and is about to drown, should there be a branch of a tree to hand, you may throw it to her that she may clutch it and save herself. Otherwise, she must drown, even though you can stretch out your hand and pull her to the bank.

Notice how all these rules are designed to subject the body and all natural feelings to the discipline of the mind. Hunger, weariness, anger, love, all had to be subdued. It was a hard life, too hard, in fact, to be popular, and it was not long before some of the rules were relaxed. Later, for example, monasteries were built and, with a roof over their heads and the consolations of a well-organised community, the monks found life easier. Each monk was allowed three robes, a loin cloth, a begging bowl, a water filter, a razor and a needle. But although physical conditions were easier, within the monasteries the object still remained the same: to exchange the world and its sufferings for the inner life of the mind. The discipline therefore continued to be severe. These were the basic rules:

A monk (1) must not harm any living thing
(2) he must not take what is not given
(3) he must not be unchaste
(4) he must not take intoxicants
(5) he must not lie
(6) he must not take unseasonable meals
(7) he must not dance, sing, play a musical instrument or watch plays
(8) he must not use flowers, scent, ointment or wear ornaments
(9) he must not use a raised bed or a wide bed
(10) he must not accept gold or silver.

## King Asoka

How did Buddhism, which began as a small sect of 'holy men', grow into a great international religion? The principal reason is that Buddhism changed its character – in some parts of the world almost beyond recognition – and became a popular religion for the masses. Long before this, however, Buddhism might well have disappeared altogether but for the dynamic influence of one man.

His name was King Asoka and he lived in India in the third century B.C. In the early years of his reign he had little interest in Buddhism. He was an excellent soldier and by successful military campaigns conquered most of India. Then, strangely enough, he was suddenly overwhelmed with remorse about the terrible sufferings inflicted on innocent people by his armies. He met some followers of Buddha and was converted. From then onwards he gave up fighting and directed his great energies to spreading the Buddhist faith.

Monasteries began to appear over the countryside and Buddhist missionaries carried the faith in all directions, throughout India and to Ceylon, Burma, Siam, and Tibet. On rocks and pillars the King inscribed the moral teaching of Buddha: that Buddhists must live at peace with all men, care for all living creatures, be truthful and honest, and revere parents and relatives. Many of these inscriptions are still to be seen in India today. Asoka himself for a time wore the robes of a monk and kept the monastic laws.

He was a delightful person to meet. He treated everybody with the greatest respect, insisting on seeing personally any-one who sought his help. In fact, he believed that to keep a man waiting for an interview was an insult to him. He tried by many means to add to the happiness of all his subjects as for example, by irrigating the land, planting trees, and building hospitals.

With him came a new respect for Buddhism and its monks. Ordinary people, of course, could not achieve nirvana in one lifetime, but they could earn merit by supporting the monks, meditating upon the Buddha, and keeping the moral law, including the first five rules of the ten observed in the monas-teries. All this would earn them at least a better reincarna-tion. The Buddhist monks responded by teaching the law especially to the young. When King Asoka died men still continued to respect and support the monks, and between the ordinary people and the monasteries a happy relationship sprang up which has continued in many Buddhist countries up to the present day.

## The Larger Vehicle

Meanwhile there were continual disputes among Buddhists as to the true meaning of their religion. Was Gautama a man or a god? Was he simply a human teacher or did he possess supernatural powers? Many different sects arose out of these disputes, but finally the Buddhist world was split into two camps: those who broadly accepted the teaching as outlined here, known as the Lesser Vehicle (*Theravada Buddhism*), and those who favoured an interpretation along supernatural lines, known as the Larger Vehicle (*Mahayana Buddhism*).

You may remember that when Gautama received his revelation under the pipal tree he had two possible courses before him. He could devote the remainder of his life to seeking nirvana for himself, or he could spend it teaching his fellow-men how to reach it. He chose the unselfish course and devoted his life to mankind. It was this pity he had for his fellow-men that became the basis of the new teaching. As his purpose was to save mankind, would he not return again and again in different forms to complete his mission? Were there not other teachers who had done the same thing? Such people were henceforth known as bodhisattvas, whose spirits in and out of the flesh were continuously seeking man's salvation. It was also argued that the spirit of Gautama was eternally present to save men, if they would seek him.

We can easily see where this teaching leads. The term 'god' is not popular in Buddhism, but instead we have 'bodhisattvas' and 'eternal buddhas' that perform, in effect, the same function as gods. As Buddhism spread, it accepted the gods of other nations as bodhisattvas.

This was an extraordinary change. The reliance upon one's self which Gautama taught had become reliance upon supernatural powers. In his teaching there seems to be no place for priests, temples, and gods. Though born a Hindu, he swept them all aside as useless. Yet within a few centuries of his death they began to reappear in his name. Magnificent stupas or monuments were built to venerate his remains, and he began to assume the likeness of a god. Today, Buddhist temples, priests, and deities are strewn across Asia in bewildering number and variety.

Such a transformation is not really surprising. Monastic life is for the few; for the many there is the need for a personal relationship with God in some form or another. Just as Hinduism produced the very popular worship of Krishna, so Buddhism produced its eternal Buddhas. In China and Japan, for example, the Pure Land sects flourished. Worship centred on the Buddha Amida (Amitofo in China). Whoever put absolute trust in Amida for salvation would gain entrance at death to his Pure Land or Western Paradise. To ensure this, many worshippers would repeat continually all through their waking lives, 'Adoration to the Buddha Amida'. This formula, it was believed, would also ward off dangers and preserve good health. Access to nirvana from the Pure Land would be easy.

The Japanese, in fact, showed themselves to be remarkably inventive in their forms of Buddha worship. Countless sects and sub-sects arose from different aspects of teaching and methods of worship. Even the worship of Amida produced no less than fourteen sects in two main streams, Pure Land sects and True Pure Land sects.

This multiplication of Buddhas and Budhisatvas provoked a stern protest in the thirteenth century from a monk, Nichiren. He denounced Pure Land sects and all other deviations, declaring that there was only one Eternal Buddha and he alone should be worshipped. His teaching from the scripture known as the Lotus Sutra ('the New Testament of Japan') had great influence and it is still reflected in many Japanese sects today.

A further challenge came from Zen Buddhism which rejects all Buddha worship. It is similar to Hindu Yoga in declaring that all true enlightenment comes from within the mind. Zen Buddhists believe that the whole truth about life cannot be rightly understood by man at all but that a certain knowledge can come suddenly by a shock such as a blow on the head or a peal of laughter. Alternatively, it may come after long hours of meditation.

In a Zen monastery the discipline is severe. In a great hall, facing one another the monks sit on raised platforms in the lotus position, their legs crossed beneath them, their eyes half closed, their hands resting on their legs, palms upwards one upon the other. Long hours of meditation are guaranteed by a monk in charge who armed with a stick belabours any monk who appears to fall asleep. When not meditating the monks are either begging food or working in the monastery or on the land.

Because of its stern self-discipline Zen became very popular with the military caste in Japan. It was an excellent training for blind obedience and fearlessness, especially in the Second World War, in strange contradiction to Buddha's teaching about the sacredness of life and the need for all Buddhists to be peacemakers. The famous 'tea ceremony' in Japan with its opportunity for withdrawal from daily life also owes much to the influence of Zen. Its principles are also applied to the ceremonies of archery, fencing, painting and flower arrangement.

One of the most colourful forms of Buddhism is to be found in Tibet. This country, tucked away amidst gigantic mountain ranges, is sixteen thousand feet above sea-level. As a consequence the Tibetans have lived in mysterious isolation for centuries. Their religion is a remarkable combination of Buddhism and their former religion, Bon, in which demons as well as gods played a considerable part. Rosaries fashioned out of human bones, prayer wheels, ghost traps, oracles, monasteries hidden away in the mountains – these are the elements of a fantastic world. The supreme ruler of Tibet was the Dalai Lama who used to live in his magnificent palace, the Potala, in Llasa. The palace contains the bodies of his predecessors and the gifts received by them over many cen-

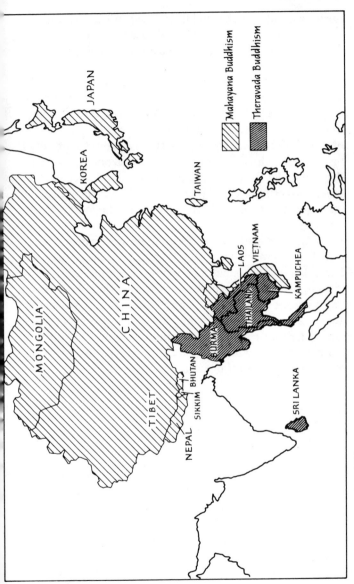

Mahayana Buddhism
Theravada Buddhism

JAPAN
KOREA
MONGOLIA
CHINA
TAIWAN
LAOS
VIETNAM
KAMPUCHEA
THAILAND
BURMA
TIBET
SIKKIM
BHUTAN
NEPAL
SRI LANKA

*The distribution of Buddhists*

turies from all over the Buddhist world. When the communists invaded Tibet in 1959 the Dalai Lama escaped to India. Since then there has been little reliable information about the country.

As Buddhism spread, its Scriptures multiplied too. The sacred books of the Larger Vehicle number thousands of volumes, which, like the Hindu Scriptures, contain something for everybody. Incredible myths began to surround the life-story of Buddha: he was miraculously born as a result of his mother's dreaming about a white elephant; when he decided under the pipal tree to serve mankind, meteors fell, mountains crumbled and rivers ran back to their source; his subsequent teaching was accompanied by the most amazing miracles.

Thus in the name of Buddhism there arose a great variety of beliefs, from the most childish superstitions to the most learned and wise conclusions about the nature of life.

Buddhism spread rapidly. In a world where lawlessness and violence were general, rulers were glad to welcome a Buddhist mission. With its moral teaching it brought peace and order into community life and it taught some men, at least, to despise wealth and accept poverty, finding within themselves the secret of eternal happiness.

# Buddhism

## 7. Buddhism today

If we examine the map of the Far East we realize what an enormous area Buddhism has covered. It is estimated that 275 million people are influenced by this religion, and three-quarters of them by the later development of the teaching known as the Larger Vehicle. Mahayana Buddhism, as it is called, is found in Japan, China, Mongolia, Korea, Tibet, Vietnam, Sikim, Bhutan and Napal. The Lesser Vehicle or Theravada Buddhism which is the older tradition dominates the countries of South East Asia; Burma, Laos, Thailand, Kampuchea and the island of Sri Lanka.

One fact to note is the early decline of Buddhism in India. After King Asoka's death, Hinduism gradually revived and its priests naturally opposed Buddhism. Then in the sixth century the White Huns invaded India and savagely destroyed hundreds of monasteries and murdered thousands of monks. Finally, from the eighth century onwards, the invasion of India by Islam had similar results. As the Buddhism of India was pacifist, we can readily understand that by the fifteenth century it had virtually disappeared.

### Buddhism in a changing world

During the last thirty years, however, Buddhism in India has realised an unusual revival. The champion of the Untouchables or Scheduled Castes was Dr. Ambedkar who died in 1956. He himself was an Untouchable who nevertheless trained in Britain as a barrister and later became law minister in the Indian government. In 1951, after four years in office, he resigned, in protest against the government's failure to safeguard the rights of his people. Before his death he became a Buddhist and encouraged his followers to take the same course. As a result more than five million Untouchables have already accepted the Buddhist faith.

In recent years Communism has spread over China and Tibet, and there is little accurate information as to what has happened to Buddhism in these countries. Communism is of course completely opposed to all forms of religion, but this does not mean that religion disappears from the countries under communist rule. Religion has a habit of surviving all the changing circumstances of human life, and no doubt in generations to come, when Marxist Communism has been replaced by some other form of government, Buddhism will still be a powerful influence in the Far East.

There is already some evidence of this influence. Just as the attempt to extinguish religious faith behind the Iron Curtain has failed, so in the Far East a similar situation has arisen. The Chinese government, rejecting the fanatical aims of the Cultural Revolution (see page 178), has found it advisable, among other things, to restore freedom to religious organisations. This has also happened in Tibet where, after invading the country, the Chinese closed the monasteries, turning the monks out to labour on the land and deported thousands of Tibetan boys to China to be trained as Communists. This policy now has been abandoned. No doubt Buddhism, which has survived many persecutions in the past, will in one form or another gradually revive in both countries.

In Japan, the love of experiment continues and new sects appear frequently. Together with Buddhism there exist two other traditional religions, Shinto and Confucianism. New ventures usually owe something to these ancient faiths. Those based on the study of the Lotus Sutra, mentioned earlier, claim the support of a fifth of the population. Soka Gakkai, as an example, has twenty million adherents. It has its own political party and seeks to build a contented nation founded on a strict sense of duty and morality. It is evangelical, seeking converts and sending missions abroad.

At the end of the Second World War, Japan became a secular state both in education and politics, but Buddhism in its many forms still claims a large following. Millions who know little about the original teaching of Gautama attend the many festivals that mark the passing of the year, as much for their social as for their religious value, and important family events are usually accompanied by Buddhist rituals.

The pacifism that is so essentially a part of Gautama's teaching seems to be in danger of disappearing in certain areas of South East Asia. In this troubled region, Buddhists have been drawn into the many struggles for freedom. In the 1970s, for example, in Vietnam, there were two movements to oust the French who dominated the country, one Communist, the other Buddhist. The Buddhists fought with great skill and but for foreign intervention might well have won. In the years following, as Communism spread, there followed an era of terrible suffering and devastation. Buddhism, nevertheless, survives today, playing a less militant role. In particular, two sects who earlier fought for freedom remain influential: the Cao Dai with its vegetarianism, care for animals, high moral values and female priests; and the Hoa Hao, teaching four main principles; patriotism, love for one's neighbour, honouring one's parents, and reverence for the scriptures. Together their followers number some millions.

A quite different political situation existed in Burma and Sri Lanka. Here, unlike Vietnam, Theravada, the older form of Buddhism, is practised. As it does not teach a belief in the supernatural, the prevailing Communism finds it less objectionable than other religions, and because of its widespread influence has tried to work in co-operation with it. The Communists argue that poverty is one of the chief causes of suffering and as Buddhism aims to end suffering, they may work together to overcome poverty. Furthermore, once the nagging need to fend off starvation is over everyone should have more time and a greater urge for meditation. So we have an experiment in social Buddhism in Burma and a Buddhist Welfare State in Sri Lanka. It does seem, however, that the final aims of Buddhism and Communism are so dissimilar that one wonders how long they can remain contented bedfellows!

In peaceful times, Buddhist monks play an important part in community life. In many countries boys spend some years in the monasteries, where they not only learn religion but also how to read and write. Their elders, too, listen to the monks as they read the Scriptures and teach a better way of life, always emphasising the five rules not to kill, to steal, to lie, to take intoxicants, or to live immorally.

Throughout Buddhist countries there are statues of the Buddha to remind people of their faith. He is usually represented seated, with close cropped hair and with long lobes to his ears. His eyes may be closed and the quiet, compassionate expression on his face is an invitation to meditate. One of the largest figures of the Buddha is in Kamakura in Japan, made of bronze thirty-nine metres high and weighing one hundred and three tons.

The pagoda or temple is another aid to meditation. People are not usually allowed inside as it may contain sacred relics but in the courtyard there are many small shrines to the Buddha – some of them perhaps privately owned – which help the Buddhist to concentrate on the teaching of 'The Enlightened One' and resolve to live a better life himself. Here he will repeat the threefold Refuge Formula (Tritatna):

I go to the Buddha for refuge,
I go to the Dhamma (the teaching) for refuge,
I go to the Sangha (the monks) for refuge.

Then, after meditating and making his private vows, he will go away, leaving behind him a present which may be money, flowers, gold leaf – whatever he thinks most suitable.

One of the finest pagodas in the world is in Rangoon, the Shwe Dagon. Its golden spires, which rise higher than St.

Paul's Cathedral are covered with gold leaf. It is constantly being renewed by Buddhists who believe that by giving gold leaf to the Temple they gain merit for the next life. Pagodas in China, however, are not temples. These beautiful, many storeyed shrines cover the relics of saints, though under a Communist regime many have fallen into ruins.

In Japan, Buddhist temples are built either of stone or in the Chinese style of black wooden pillars supporting a roof with upturned eaves. People come daily in large numbers to worship before the altar on which may rest an image of the Amida Buddha. They will listen to readings from the scriptures and to a sermon and afterwards may drink tea together before they go home. Some temples hold special festivals during the year, the most important being the celebration of Gautama's birthday on 8 April. Many of the modern sects in Japan have their own festival days marked by great crowds worshipping fervently the Buddha or bodhisattva in whom they believe. In the home also there will be a shrine with an image or silk painting surrounded by flowers and lights. On the shrine may be a tablet commemorating the family's ancestors and with it portions of the scriptures. Each morning an act of worship and meditation will be followed by the lighting of a stick of incense. Today, in some parts of the Far East, there is great political unrest, and we read of Buddhist monks taking an active part in the settling of social and political problems. It is possible therefore as life changes in these countries, the role of the monk will change with it.

Buddhism is a missionary religion and in recent years it has spread into Europe. In 1924 a Buddhist Lodge was established in England and in 1928 in France. Buddhism has also a firm foothold in America, though this is not due to missions but to the emigration of great numbers of Chinese and Japanese in the nineteenth century. The Buddhist Church of America is Mahayana in doctrine but also reflects western and Christian influences. Buddhists have been particularly concerned about the failure of Christianity to prevent warfare.

They believe that Buddhist teaching on pacifism and reverence for all life is very much needed in the world today.

## Buddhism and the human mind

Has Buddhism, then, something of real value for the Western world? Its moral teaching – pacifism, honesty, truthfulness, sobriety, faithfulness in marriage, compassion for all men – is greatly needed everywhere among individuals and nations. On the other hand, much of Buddhist practice and belief would be summarily dismissed as superstition: bodhisattvas, gods offering private paradises to their worshippers, incantations, sacred formulae – none of these could survive the modern scientific outlook on life. It is doubtful, too, if many people could accept the Four Noble Truths (p 34). Gautama appears to have believed that it was a mistake that man ever inhabited this planet. Life here is a disaster: therefore we must get rid of it. The Western attitude is different. Whatever may be man's future life, this world is our temporary home and we should make the most of it. In doing so, we hope to achieve happiness.

It is on this idea of happiness that modern Buddhism would challenge us. Many people speak and act as if happiness in life is measured in money. The sole purpose of education, they assume, is a good job and good money. Great nations reflect this view: it is their wealth that makes them great and by continually raising standards of living they expect to make their people happier. Buddhism maintains, however, that such reasoning is false: our true standard of living is not measured in motor-cars and TV sets but simply in the state of our minds. 'Nothing is but thinking makes it so.' Happiness is a mental condition dependent on what we train ourselves to think and feel.

This point of view should not be lightly brushed aside. It is a sobering fact that among the most well-to-do nations we find steadily increasing numbers of people who are mentally and emotionally disturbed. Despite their prosperity they find life empty and void of the deep satisfaction we all yearn for. The strain of living from day to day is too much for them; they cannot cope with life's problems.

We should not be at all surprised at this, declares Buddhism, because the root of our unhappiness lies in material possessions and our craving for them. Perhaps this is also what Jesus of Nazareth meant when he spoke of 'the deceitfulness of riches'. The Buddhist answer to this widespread problem is to offer a mental discipline which would limit our desires and make us content with a much simpler way of life. But more important still, Buddhism declares that as we look within ourselves, we shall find there a peace and contentment that nothing in the external world can give us. This is a claim made by other religions too, as, for example, the highest form of Hinduism and Christianity which offers 'that peace which the world cannot give'.

In order to find this inner serenity, an educated Buddhist will put aside an hour or more a day for meditation. By continual practise he is able to cut himself off from the world around him and to rise to a higher plane of existence, free from thought, pain, worry, and the tense problems of life. When, at length, he returns to normal life, he feels a new creature, mentally alert and self-controlled. He is in harmony with his fellow men and ready to be of service to them.

In many other religions the practise of meditation produces similar results. Nor should we be surprised at this when we recognize what enormous spiritual and mental powers lie buried within us. The human mind has resources that we seldom use in our daily life. For example, it can be trained to remember 'forgotten' facts; to behave as an alarm clock, waking us at any hour of the night we choose; to perform remarkable feats of memory as in the case of Muslim children who can recite 114 chapters of the Qur'an; to remain cheerful in the face of misfortune. It certainly has far more influence on our bodily health than is generally recognized.

The understanding and control of the mind, then, is all-important to us. If you feel satisfied with your own ability in this respect, try a short experiment. Place a simple object before you and concentrate your thought upon it for, say, three minutes without allowing your mind to wander. You will probably discover that you have far less control over your mind than you have over your body.

It is to the mind, then, that the Buddhist would have us turn for the solution of life's problems: firstly, because peace is to be found within its hidden depths – remember the statues of Buddha with closed eyes and a gentle smile upon his face; secondly, because by meditation we acquire a mental discipline that saves us from the stress of modern living and keeps us always in harmony with the world around us. Together with its moral teaching, these claims make Buddhism of special interest to a civilization in which so many people are restless and unhappy.

# From the Buddhist Scriptures

All that we are is the result of what we have thought: it is founded on our thoughts, it is made up of our thoughts. A tamed mind brings happiness.

(*Dhammapada*)

He who, seeking his own happiness, punishes or kills beings who also long for happiness, will not find happiness after death.

(*Dhammapada*)

Let a man overcome anger by love, let him overcome evil by good; let him overcome the greedy by liberality, the liar by truth.

(*Dhammapada*)

The greatest wealth consisteth in being charitable. And the greatest happiness in having tranquillity of mind.

(Tibetan Sayings)

'Look at evil as evil' is the first *dhamma* teaching. 'Seeing evil as evil, be disgusted therewith, be cleansed of it, be freed of it' is the second *dhamma* teaching.

(Gautama)

# Points for discussion

1. 'The root cause of suffering is desire.' Do you consider that wanting things is a major cause of unhappiness? Is it better to be always ambitious for something that lies just beyond our grasp or should we learn to be content with what we have?

2. Read again the paragraph on speech, conduct, and employment (p 35). Do you think that the directions there would be a useful guide for everybody?

3 The practice of Buddhism begins with learning to control the mind. Consider in how many different ways we can learn to control our thinking and our emotions.

4 Why do you think the later development of Buddhism introduced priests, temples, and bodhisattvas?

5 What useful part can monasteries play in the life of mankind?

# Confucianism

## 8. The Primal Sage of China

In the year that Gautama, the founder of Buddhism, was born in a royal palace on the slopes of the Himalayas, a poor boy was playing in the streets of his native village two thousand miles away. He was destined to become as famous in China as Gautama became in India. His name was K'ung Chin, but when as a man he became a great teacher, his followers spoke of him as K'ung Futzu or Master Kung. Centuries later a Jesuit missionary latinized the word as 'Confucius', and by this name he has been known in the Western world ever since.

### The tragic condition of China

When in 551 B.C. Confucius was born, China was in a state of turmoil. From the eleventh century B.C. the Chou family had been rulers over northern China. The head of the family was the god-Emperor, the mighty 'Son of Heaven'. But as the country was so vast, much of the land was shared out among his relatives and a kind of feudal system existed. In the time of Confucius, however, this system had broken down. Barbarians were invading the land, and in addition the nobles were fighting among themselves for power and wealth. The Emperor had ceased to have any real influence. For example, the state of Lu (now known as Shantung), in which Confucius was born, had been invaded over twenty times in two hundred years.

When petty tyrants rampage about the countryside, the chief sufferers are always the poor. The peasants of China were little more than serfs, and nobles passing over their land would steal timber, grain, and cattle according to the whim of the moment, mutilating or killing anyone unwise enough to protest. Torture, in fact, was almost a pastime. Mutilation of the feet was so common that shops sold special footgear to assist the victims. Everywhere the common people suffered. In the siege of the capital of Sung in 593 B.C. the citizens were driven in desperation to eat their children, first exchanging them between families to avoid parents' devouring their own offspring.

This state of lawlessness seems even more tragic when we realise how clever and progressive the Chinese really were. A thousand years before Caesar met the woad-dyed warriors of Britain, the Chinese had their walled cities, their art, science, commerce, and philosophy. The theory of evolution was taught in China three thousand years before it dawned upon the West. In those remote days the Chinese were writing in ink on wood, bamboo, and silk. Sunspots were observed sixteen centuries before Galileo recorded them in Europe, and in the fifth century B.C. astronomers had already calculated the year to consist of $365\frac{1}{4}$ days. Water-clocks were invented in the second century B.C., dividing each day into a hundred equal parts. Within their splendid cities the Chinese built magnificent palaces, temples, and mausoleums. No wonder they often thought of foreigners as barbarians.

## *The life of Confucius*

Confucius's parents were poor and early in life he became an orphan. He married at nineteen but of his home life we know little. He had a son and two daughters. His wife, we are told, was a rather impractical young woman who distressed both her husband and her neighbours by persistently playing the lute in the early hours of the morning, and finally ran away from home. The marriage was evidently not a happy one.

From an early age Confucius, a quiet and studious young man, showed distress at his country's plight and determined to devote his life to putting it right. He travelled about from state to state, talking to rulers, studying manuscripts, and gathering about him a group of young men to whom he taught the art of government. He found many rulers willing to listen to him, but none prepared to give him power to put his teaching into practice.

So he returned to Lu. There, to his delight, he was first appointed Minister for Crime and later Prime Minister. He was remarkably successful. He established peace, fed and clothed the poor, freed the countryside from highwaymen, built bridges, repaired roadways, and developed trade. The people responded with hard work and Lu became exceedingly prosperous.

But Lu's prosperity awakened the jealousy of her neighbours, and one ruler hit upon an ingenious plan to upset Confucius. He made a gift to the Duke of Lu of eighty pretty girls and one hundred and twenty magnificent horses. The girls were as high-spirited as the horses, and, being well instructed in the role they were to play, made such an impact on the Court of Lu that Duke and ministers alike forgot their duties, their engagements, and themselves in a prolonged and riotous carnival. The festive spirit swept through the countryside, and the people, overtaxed with hard work and sober living, followed their ruler's example. The last state of Lu was worse than the first. Confucius departed in disgust.

For thirteen years he travelled from province to province but he never found anyone else who would give him power. He was greatly disappointed and despaired of China's rulers. 'Rotten wood,' he declared sadly, 'cannot be carved.'

For the last time he returned to Lu and settled in a peaceful valley where for five years he wrote and taught his followers. At the age of seventy-three he died. He was buried on the banks of the river Lu, and his grave is approached today through a magnificent gateway and an avenue of trees. On a marble slab are inscribed the words, 'Confucius, the Primal Sage'.

Confucius, like many other famous men, had great personal charm. He treated rich and poor alike, would greet the humblest visitor with genuine delight, and listen attentively to whatever he had to say. He was always tolerant, wishing neither to assert himself nor to deride those who did not agree with him.

He showed both moral and physical courage. The rulers he met were powerful men, but he never hesitated to say what he thought was right, however much he might suffer as a consequence. He had no time for the man who treats his inferiors with contempt and on the other hand is servile to his superiors. He was often in physical danger as he travelled through the lawless countryside. When his disciples were afraid, he would sit down by the roadside, play on his stringed instrument, and sing cheerful songs until their courage revived.

He was completely absorbed in his work. On one occasion a disciple, when asked about his master's character, found difficulty in summing it up. When Confucius heard of it he exclaimed, 'Why did you not reply: "He is a man who learns truth without growing weary, who instructs mankind without becoming disgusted, who is so zealous that he forgets his food, who is so joyous that he forgets all care, and so does not observe the gradual approach of old age"?'

## The teaching of Confucius

Some time after Confucius's death a disciple called Mencius (Meng-tsu) and his friends wrote a number of volumes on the teaching of Confucius. The most important is a small collection of discussions and sayings called *The Analects*. Though Mencius added ideas of his own to these works, they contain for the most part what Confucius himself taught.

Unlike other religious teachers Confucius taught nothing about God. He accepted the religious beliefs of his day, taking a delight in all the ceremonies they involved. He also spoke about 'Heaven' as having sent him and preserving him in his work. The Chinese showed great reverence for their ancestors and in every home there were wooden plaques, each giving the name and dates of past members of the family. They believed that their ancestors were always present in spirit to guide them through life. Confucius accepted this belief and encouraged the elaborate ceremonies connected with it.

Confucius, however, wanted most of all to save his countrymen from ruin, and he believed that this could be done by education. Men did evil, he thought, because they were ignorant of what was good. Teach them what is good and they would live in harmony with the rest of creation. He therefore set out by education to produce the perfect man – 'the gentleman' – and, in particular, to train his followers to become expert ministers of state whom rulers would employ to restore order in their realms.

It is Confucius's ideas on education that are perhaps most valuable today. The aim of education was not to pass examinations. To spend years of one's life collecting and memorising facts so that on a given day on a given piece of paper they could be scribbled down in a given number of minutes would be no proof of an educated man. Nor was the object of education to gain a good position and a good wage. The most successful schools, in Confucius's mind, would be those that turned out a stream of unselfish, high-minded, public-spirited young people. The study of books and the learning of special skills were both necessary, but were useless, if not dangerous, unless the pupil's character was also trained.

What qualities, therefore, did Confucius produce in his followers? First of all, self-control. No one had the right to govern others until he had learnt to govern himself. This is perhaps the most important problem in life for everybody, for when a man can control his thoughts and actions he is well on the way to happiness, whatever his social position may be. Confucius insisted that his pupils were polite to everyone. Young and old, rich and poor, friend and foe, all were to be treated with equal courtesy. This, at least, was a good beginning in self-control for a man who was subject to changing moods and tempers. A man should watch himself, too, when he was not in company, for character is formed more when we are alone than when we are with others. Confucius disliked babblers. A man should speak only when he has something worthwhile to say. But he should be resolute in action. He should be capable of weighing up the facts of any situation, able to make up his mind and pursue a course of action despite opposition, if he knew it to be right.

His pupils therefore must be self-reliant. They must learn to think for themselves. He once declared, 'I can't teach a man who is not trying to make things clear to himself. If I explain one quarter and the man does not go away and think out for himself the remaining three-quarters, I won't bother to teach him.'

At the same time a pupil must guard against pride. Confucius himself was a constant example of humility. 'Whenever I walk with two companions,' he said, 'I can always find one who has something to teach me.' He did not care for the man who was always criticising other people. One of his pupils had this weakness and Confucius quaintly remarked about him, 'Obviously Tze-Kiung has become quite perfect himself to have time to spare for this. I do not have this much leisure.'

Confucius knew nothing of democracy and he taught obedience: the son obedient to his father; the father, to the ruler of the state. But he said plainly that no ruler should be allowed to govern at all unless his aim was to make his people happy. The family was all-important. Children should never cause anxiety to their parents except by unavoidable illness. Through the kindness and courtesy practised in individual families the whole nation would be gradually transformed and state control would largely disappear. Confucius did not talk about foreigners as barbarians: he said that all men were brothers and hoped that his teaching would go far beyond the bounds of China.

## The later developments of Confucianism

Confucius would no doubt have been amazed to see the effects of his teaching on China, for he died a disappointed man. But his followers were far more successful than he had been. They proved to be expert ministers of state and it was not long before rulers everywhere were seeking their services. All through the centuries when China became the greatest nation on earth and later when she kept aloof and lived in secret isolation, the influence of Confucius dominated her way of life. His teaching also spread to Japan, where it still remains a powerful influence.

Yet Confucius did not achieve his supreme ambition: the education of all his fellow-countrymen. There were many reasons for this failure. In the first place, Buddhism and Tao, the two other religions of China, affected Confucianism so that Confucius tended to become a divine being, the worship of whom supplanted the practice of his teaching. Then Confucianism began to emphasise class differences. Examinations were held in the teaching of Confucius and these became so difficult that only people who could devote all their time to study could hope to pass them. Thus the workers and the poor were excluded. Thirdly, with the rise of democracy, Confucianism was linked in people's minds with the old imperial system. In 1911, therefore, when economic and political difficulties brought the downfall of the Emperor, Confucianism fell with him.

In 1949 came another great change. The People's Republic of China was officially established and Communism began to claim the Chinese for an entirely new way of life.

In 1966 Chairman Mao Tse-Tung organised a Cultural Revolution, mainly to revive the interest of Chinese youth in the progress of Communism. Among other things it aimed to root out all religious faith and activity, but on the death of Mao, after a struggle for power, a more liberal government succeeded and interest in religion revived. The Chinese wish

63

to preserve their ancient traditions and Confucius is now honoured for his concern for the individual, especially for the poor, and is represented as an early teacher of democracy!

Perhaps what is really good in Confucianism is on its way back to claim its rightful place in the future of China, and the Primal Sage may yet prove to be 'the teacher of ten thousand generations'.

# Sayings of Confucius

What you do not wish others to do to you, do not unto them.

Reading without thinking gives a disorderly mind and thinking without reading makes one unbalanced.

Among the truly educated there is no distinction of classes.

Poetry will stimulate your emotions, help you to be more observant, enlarge your sympathies, and moderate your resentment of justice.

Do not be concerned because you are not in office, but with making yourself qualified for office; do not be concerned that you are unknown but with being worthy of reputation.

No man can hide his character. Look closely into his aims, observe the means by which he pursues them, and discover what brings him content.

Stay far from clever talkers for they are dangerous.

It is goodness that gives a neighbourhood its beauty.

The things that trouble and concern me are the following: lest I should neglect to improve my character, lest I should neglect my studies, and lest I should fail to move forward when I see the right course or fail to correct myself when I see my mistake.

With coarse food to eat and water to drink and with no pillow but my bent arm, I can still find happiness. Riches and honour acquired by unrighteousness are to me as a floating cloud.

# Points for discussion

1 In education Confucius put character-training first. He thought it most important to produce unselfish, high-minded, and public-spirited young people. What do you think should be the chief aim of education?

2 Do you think that democracy is the most effective form of government? Has Confucius's idea of government by a wise and benevolent ruler advantages over democracy?

# Taoism

## 9. The quiet life

During the sixth century B.C. five of the greatest religious teachers were alive: Buddha, Confucius, Lao-tze, Mahavira, and Zoroaster. The third of these Lao-tze, was the founder of Taoism (pronounced Dow-ism), a religion that for two thousand years helped to mould the character of the Chinese people.

### *The origin of Taoism*

Very little is known about the life of Lao-tze, and parts of the traditional story are obviously mythical.

Li Uhr – for that was Lao-tze's real name – was born on a farm in the province of Honan in 604 B.C. At birth he was said to have been white-haired and seventy-two years old. Because of this surprising fact he was nicknamed Lao-tze, which means 'Old Boy' or 'Old Master'. He became librarian at the court of a local ruler, where he was famed for his wisdom. While he was there he met Confucius, whose teaching he despised. 'Go home,' he said to him, 'and give up your proud airs and many desires.'

Lao-tze did not like court life. Everyone there was concerned about money, fame, and power, and the state was corrupt. So one day he mounted a cart driven by two black oxen and made for the western mountains. At the city gate the guard recognized him and begged him to halt his journey long enough to write down his philosophy of life. Thereupon Lao-tze wrote his famous book in five thousand Chinese characters. Then taking to his ox-cart again he continued his journey. It was said that far away on a mountain pass he disappeared into a cloud. Whatever happened, he was never seen again.

Some scholars doubt whether such a person as Lao-tze ever lived. This does not, in fact, matter very much as it is the book and not the life of its author that is important. This book is entitled the *Tao-te-ching* (pronounced Dow-du-Jing), which translated means *The Book of the Way and its Power*.

## *The* Tao

Lao-tze sets out to answer the question that everyone at some time asks, 'What is really at the heart of the universe?' If we could see behind the appearance of things, if we could go backstage and discover how the play which we call Life is produced in this world, what should we learn? Lao-tze says that the answer is to be found in the one word *Tao*. This word is variously translated as the Way, the Path, or the Origin of everything. The meaning is difficult because the *Tao* cannot be defined. Its true nature will always remain 'darker than any mystery', but there are some things that we do know about it.

*Tao* is not a god but a force or a principle that overflows all things. It loves and nourishes, but it neither meddles nor seeks to possess anything. It works gently and quietly and without effort, and everything that has to be done is done efficiently. Consider, as an example, the progress of nature through the year. The four seasons in unvarying order merge one into the other almost unnoticed. Yet in each season nature fulfils her duties completely and efficiently without worry or bustle. In this manner the *Tao* presides silently and efficiently over all things.

Lao-tze then goes on to say that if a man wishes to be content he must live his life in a similar way. 'There is no greater calamity than not to be contented.' Man needs to live in harmony with the *Tao* and must therefore seek its qualities. His life must be orderly and unhurried, his actions quiet and controlled. In his relations with others he is a man of peace. He does not desire to dominate, interfere, or to possess. War is so far from his nature that he cannot even admire

68

warlike instruments. In all disputes he prefers to talk things over. Like the Buddhist he respects all life, human, animal, and insect. He is humble and gentle, and influences people without appearing to do so. There is no better example for the man of *Tao* than that of water. Water benefits all men. Yet it is gentle, acting quietly, overcoming all things and seeking always the lowest place, a position which men normally despise.

Government in Lao-tze's day was unjust and oppressive, and Lao-tze regarded it as evil and unnecessary. It was the cause of a continuous struggle for power, wealth, and privilege, and the common man was always the sufferer. Let men alone, he said, cease to meddle in their lives, and they will be naturally good and happy.

Here we can see why Lao-tze disliked Confucius. Confucius believed that China could be reformed by the appointment of good rulers and by educating the people. Lao-tze valued neither. Contentment and peace would come only when men contemplated the *Tao* and lived their lives in harmony with it.

One of the best-known teachers of *Tao* was Chuang Tzu (369–286 B.C.). He was a philosopher and a mystic. He doubted the existence of the world which we perceive through our five senses. How real was it? He describes how one day he dreamt that he was a butterfly fluttering about joyfully from flower to flower. Then he awoke. 'Now,' said he, 'I do not know whether I was then a man dreaming I was a butterfly or whether I am now a butterfly dreaming that I am a man.' True knowledge did not come from outside ourselves but from within, by contemplating the *Tao*.

Here we have the mysticism common to many religions. The object in Taoism was union with the *Tao*, and the method is not unlike what we read about in Buddhism. There were four stages. First the 'holy man' retired into solitude, then he practised abstinence, which leads to vision and understanding, and finally he was brought to ecstatic union with the *Tao*. He then possessed the qualities of the *Tao*, and men would naturally accept him as their teacher and follow him.

Also connected with Taoism was the *Yin-Yang* theory. It was believed that there were five agents in the world: water, fire, wood, metal, and soil. Through these agents two principles operated: the *Yin*, which was negative and feminine, cold, dark, soft, moist, and changeable; and the *Yang*, which was positive and masculine, warm, bright, firm, dry, and steadfast. The interaction of these two principles produced all the activity of heaven and earth. 'One *Yin* and one *Yang* is the *Tao*,' it was said.

## The decline of Taoism

Though there was much in the work of the *Tao* philosophers to encourage the good and contented life, it was never free from superstition. Sound advice such as, 'obey your parents; do not use a light balance or a small pint', is mixed up with such nonsense as 'do not spit towards the north; do not point at a rainbow'. Unfortunately, the superstition gradually replaced the common sense.

It was not long before the usual priesthood and temples began to appear. Gods and nature spirits multiplied, and the departed saints were said to inhabit the mythical 'Islands of the Blest'. Celestial teachers or 'popes' arose who were believed to know the secrets of winning immortality. They levied taxes on their followers and lived in comfort themselves on sacred mountains. Taoist priests, in modern times, have become little more than workers of magic, able, it is believed, to drive away evil spirits, to bring down the rain, and produce pills and formulae to cure diseases and ensure long life.

Already a change is coming, however. With the development of education this morass of magic and superstition is being swept away. It will leave behind the writings of Lao-tze and his earliest followers. From the turmoil of the twentieth century the Chinese may turn again for the tranquil life to the Book of *Tao* and its excellent moral teaching.

# Shinto

## 10. Shrines and sects

Shinto is the Buddhist name for the ancient religion of Japan. When eager missionaries arrived in Japan in the sixth century with Buddha's 'Way of Deliverance', they had to coin a name for the religion that they found there. So they called it *Shen-tao*, 'The Way of the Gods', for the Japanese worshipped hundreds of gods: the great nature gods common to most primitive religions and the spirits that were believed to inhabit the mountains, trees, rivers, and every other special feature of the Japanese countryside.

*Shen-tao*, or Shinto as we call it in the West, is therefore not a world religion like Buddhism or Christianity, but merely a general term for the ancient religion of Japan and what remains of it today. It takes two forms: Shrine Shinto, from which State Shinto developed, and Sect Shinto.

### Shrine Shinto

It is believed that in Japan there are over one hundred thousand shrines. In their earliest form shrines were plots of ground considered holy because they were the dwelling-places of the gods. Gradually they acquired buildings until today they are very similar in pattern everywhere. The most impressive are those out in the open country or by the sea, where the grounds adjoining them may occupy many square miles.

The visitor begins his approach to a shrine by passing under an archway known as a *torii*. The upright posts lean slightly towards each other and are surmounted by two beams, the upper one usually being the longer. These *torii* indicate to the visitor that he is passing from his everyday world into the very sacred presence of his god. He will probably find water by the archway with which he should wash his hands and wash out his mouth as a sign of purification. The path to the shrine may be flanked by magnificent tall trees which together with the beauty of the countryside create an atmosphere of grandeur and peace. At night lanterns light up the roadway.

Presently the visitor reaches the Hall of Worship. This is a building supported by a number of pillars. It is not used by the public, but on important occasions special ceremonies are conducted there.

Finally, he arrives at the shrine itself. This is always built above ground-level and is therefore approached up a number of broad steps. It consists usually of a single room built of unpainted timber. Its roof, which may be thatched, has wide overhanging gables. Within it is concealed some object sacred to the god, possibly a mirror, a sword, a lock of hair, a piece of cloth, or some consecrated paper. No one enters the shrine save the priests. The way into it is barred by a rope of thick-plaited straw from which protrude pieces of cloth and paper. There is also a wooden or bamboo pole which is a symbol of the divine presence.

The worshipper stands before the shrine, bows reverently, claps his hands together, rings a bell to inform the god (Kami) of his presence, recites some sacred verse, says his own prayers, makes an offering of money or rice, and then leaves. The whole ceremony is in harmony with the atmosphere of dignity and peace which envelopes the shrine.

Japan is a country of many festivals. On important occasions crowds assemble at the shrines to witness the performance of elaborate rituals by the priests. At some of the larger shrines they may also see pantomimes or dances and there may be a procession in which a portable shrine is carried on a huge float around the neighbourhood to symbolise a journey of the god whom it represents. Priests sell charms or may foretell the future and are consulted for this purpose like the oracles and augurs of Greece and Rome.

In recent years, perhaps due to the influence of other religions, the Japanese have been encouraged to celebrate family events at a shrine. For example, there are now ceremonies for the naming of children and for both marriages and funerals, though funerals are more often attended by Buddhist priests.

Workers in the fields or in factories may have small shrines where they worship a deity whom they feel will bless the kinds of work they are doing. In the town, shrines are confined to much smaller spaces than in the country, but the smallest shrines are in the home. Here on a 'god-shelf' high up on the wall, symbols of the family's ancestors are enclosed in small cupboards. Before them, as with the great shrines, is a straw-plaited rope. Food and flowers are placed before the shrine and prayers are said there daily.

*Sect Shinto*

Shrine worship dates back to antiquity. Though it suffered a serious blow as a result of the Second World War, it will probably continue to be the basis of Japanese religious life. During the last century, however, many Japanese felt the additional need for congregational worship. So, perhaps as a result of Christian and Buddhist influences, Shinto also expresses itself in the form of churches and religious communities known as sects.

You may recall that there are many Buddhist sects in Japan. In addition, a fifth of the population belong to Shinto sects. Some of them single out one of the ancient gods and worship him as the supreme deity; others are based on Confucian teaching. There are also sects that have little connection with the old religions. Two of the most important, founded in the nineteenth century, believe in faith-healing. Of these 'the Religion of the Divine Reason' is very like Christian Science. Its founder, Maekawa-Miki, with her family, suffered severe illness and only recovered health at last by religious faith. She then gave away all her wealth and practised divine healing. In a trance it was revealed to her that disease arose from the following sins: covetousness, meanness, undisciplined love, hatred, revenge, anger, pride and selfishness. The object of the church is twofold: to cleanse the mind of these sins, and to work actively to overcome sickness and poverty and to establish peace on earth. This sect is the largest in Japan with ten thousand temples and between four and five million members.

Sects are tolerated by the Japanese government, provided their teaching does not run counter to basic political beliefs. We shall see the importance of this proviso as we study State Shinto.

## State Shinto

The greatest of all the Shinto gods is Amaterasu, and her shrine at Isé is the most important one in Japan. At this shrine are preserved a great mirror and sword, famous because they undoubtedly are very old and are connected with Japanese stories of creation and the giving of light to the earth.

Amaterasu is the sun-goddess. It is said that her son married the god that inhabits *Fuji-yama*, Japan's sacred mountain, and that their grandson became the first Emperor of Japan. The foundation of the Japanese Empire is dated at 660 B.C., and so it is now over 2,600 years old. Up to the end of the Second World War it was claimed that the Emperor of Japan, the Mikado, was descended directly from the sun-goddess, and he was worshipped as divine.

From time to time during its long history Shinto has been affected by foreign religions, especially Buddhism. Buddhist priests, for instance, took over the care of many shrines, and Buddhist images began to appear in them. But the Japanese in their island home have always had a strong national consciousness, which expresses itself in periods of strong anti-foreign feeling. Between 1624 and 1868 Japan tried to exclude all foreign influence and to live entirely to herself.

74

Both Buddhism and Christianity were severely persecuted, and a purified Shinto was considered the only true religion. In the second half of the nineteenth century relations with other countries had to be reopened, and both Buddhism and Christianity revived. But the fervent nationalists in Japan were quite determined that whatever other religions flourished in their country, the basic faith of their people should be pure Shinto.

So State Shinto arose. The government sought control of the shrines and over three hundred were directly operated by them. At these shrines the Japanese paid homage to past emperors and other great men who had served their country, including war heroes. Children in school were required to learn the names of 124 god-emperors. Portraits of the Emperor appeared everywhere and obeisance had to be made to them. All great public ceremonies connected with the Emperor were conducted at a shrine and their main purpose was to encourage absolute devotion to both Emperor and Nation.

The government was rather careful to hide this fervent patriotism from representatives of foreign nations. They were allowed to see all the pageantry but were not informed of its real meaning for the Japanese people. Other religions, such as Buddhism and Christianity, were tolerated. But in practice, especially before the Second World War, the government's real aim was to foster a conviction that the Japanese were the greatest nation on earth and that the Emperor should eventually extend his dominion over all the world. This fanatical belief reached its peak during the Second World War, when, for example, Japanese airmen crashed their planes as well as their bombs into enemy targets. To die for their country would make them immortal.

### Recent developments

The Japanese suffered overwhelming defeat in the Second World War. In the Far East the war which they had begun by

75

a deadly attack on the American naval base at Pearl Harbour ended with two shattering atomic explosions on Nagasaki and Hiroshima. These two bombs not only finished the war but destroyed the power of State Shinto. All the government propaganda carefully developed over many years about Japanese invincibility disappeared overnight.

The country was occupied by the Americans. In 1945 State Shinto was disestablished: it ceased to have any further connection with the government. Henceforth it was allowed to exist only on the same terms as other forms of Shinto. The Emperor declared that he was not in fact divine, and he was deprived of any further political power. Meanwhile, ceremonies still continued at state shrines, but they were in the care of a National Shrine Association. Their purpose now was rather different – world peace and brotherhood.

After the terrible shock of defeat, the Japanese lost faith in their religion and their shrines were neglected. But gradually as the years have passed by they have flocked back to them especially for the great festivals of which the New Year is for many people the most important. It usually lasts three days, beginning at midnight on 31 December. On this occasion the Meiji Shrine in Tokyo, which honours the former emperor of that name, is visited by about three million worshippers.

Other shrines commemorate Japan's war dead and others are devoted to the god of war. So with the revival of the Shinto shrine has followed a revival of interest in Japan's past achievements and military prowess, hardly unexpected in the kind of world in which we are living today.

# From the *Tao* Scriptures

*The Eternal* Tao

There is a thing inherent and natural,
Which existed before heaven and earth.
Motionless and fathomless,
It stands alone and never changes;
It pervades everywhere and never becomes exhausted.
It may be regarded as the Mother of the Universe.
I call it *Tao*, and I name it as supreme.

*The Perfect Man of* Tao

He is cautious, like one who crosses a stream in winter;
He is hesitating, like one who fears his neighbours;
He is modest, like one who is a guest;
He is yielding, like ice that is going to melt;
He is simple, like wood that is not yet wrought;
He is vacant, like valleys that are hollow;
He is dim, like water that is turbid.

He who knows others is wise;
He who knows himself is enlightened
He who conquers others is strong;
He who conquers himself is mighty.

There has been such a thing as letting mankind alone;
There has never been such a thing as governing mankind.

Without going out of the door
One can know the whole world;
Without peeping out of the window
One can see the *Tao* of heaven.
The further one travels, the less one knows.

# Points for discussion

1 Can you think of any other religion which, like State Shinto, has been linked with the destiny of one special nation? What are the weaknesses of this kind of religion?

2 Read again what Lao-tze says about government. Do you think government interferes too much in our lives or too little? What would be the ideal relation between the people and those who govern them?

3 'There is no greater calamity than not to be contented.' Do you agree with Lao-tze's way to contentment?

# Judaism

## 11. A faith for four thousand years

One of the most ancient of living religions is Judaism, the religion of the Jews. It began about four thousand years ago when there appeared near the eastern shores of the Mediterranean a race of people known as Hebrews, and later as Israelites. They inhabited the country of Canaan, a word meaning 'The Land of Purple', for at that time the shellfish along its shores were used to produce a famous purple dye.

Eventually, Canaan became known as Palestine, 'the Land of the Philistines', and the Israelites were called Jews. Not all the descendants of the Israelites, however, became Jews. Very early in their history the Israelites were divided into twelve tribes named after the sons of the patriarch, Jacob. Many centuries later, as a nation, they were conquered and taken into captivity. While exiled from Palestine, ten of the twelve tribes disappeared and only two, Benjamin and Judah, eventually returned. It is the descendants of these two surviving tribes that are the Jews today.

### The remarkable faith of the Jews

Though there are about thirteen and a half million Jews scattered throughout the world (nearly half of them in the U.S.A.) few people have accurate knowledge of their way of life. Who, for example, could describe the religious beliefs and customs of a modern Jewish household? A number of reasons may account for this ignorance. Judaism is not a missionary religion; inter-marriage with Gentiles (non-Jews) is rare; and dietary laws and other customs tend to separate them from other people. Persecution, too, has added to their

79

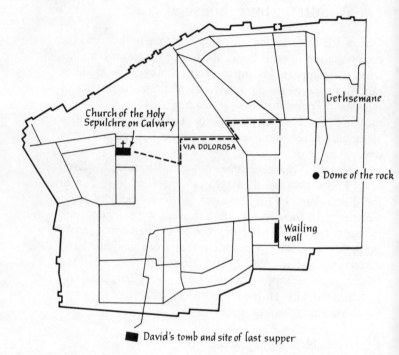

Church of the Holy
Sepulchre on Calvary

VIA DOLOROSA

Gethsemane

● Dome of the rock

Wailing
wall

■ David's tomb and site of last supper

*Jerusalem*

*The Sacred City of three religions;*
*Judaism, Christianity, and Islam*

NB *The Dome of the Rock* is the traditional site
from which Muhammad ascended to heaven
and where two hairs from the Prophet's head are preserved

isolation. They have learnt through bitter experience to live to themselves. From the remote days of their slavery in Egypt down to modern times they have been the most persecuted race on earth, suffering martyrdom in millions, mainly at the hands of ignorant ruffians. And in the twentieth century their sufferings have been worse than at any other time in their unhappy history.

Nevertheless, they have held stubbornly to their faith in God. This remarkable faith, though we hear little about it today, greatly impressed the ancient world, attracting the wise and learned of other races, and making many converts. Moreover, as the old pagan beliefs proved useless and died, Judaism survived and laid the foundations of two other great world religions, Christianity and Islam.

Why did Judaism survive and play so remarkable a role in history? When Titus, the son of the Emperor Vespasian, took Jerusalem in A.D. 70, one of his first acts, when the city surrendered, was to find the Temple, and tear aside the veil covering the Holy of Holies. With his own eyes he wanted to gaze upon the secret God of the Jews. His curiosity was shared by other Gentiles. Some who ridiculed the Jews spread the rumour that there was an ass's head behind the veil. Yet Titus found nothing; no idol, no image, no peculiar or mysterious object of worship, nothing but a few relics of their ancient life in the desert. To him it seemed unbelievable that in a world full of idols there could exist a nation without one. Yet for many hundreds of years this had been so. The Jews had been taught that there was but one God, invisible, righteous, and loving, and the sole creator of the universe.

The belief that God is spiritual is shared by many people today. What, however, is remarkable is that the Jews realized it so many centuries before it dawned on the minds of other people. In this and in other ways they were far in advance of the nations around them and may well claim to be called God's Chosen People, a race specially selected to reveal his true nature to the world.

*Their early history*

The beginning of the Christian era divides the four thousand years of Jewish history into two equal parts. The earlier period (B.C.E. Before Christian era) is much better known to non-Jews than the later one (C.E. Christian era). It is largely described in the Jewish sacred books known as *The Law, the Prophets, and the Writings*, but known to non-Jews as the Old Testament, the first part of the Christian Bible.

It is the story of a determined little nation fighting to preserve its faith and its territory from the constant bullying of more powerful neighbours. Even when defeated, enslaved, or exiled, the Israelites still maintained their spiritual independence, convinced that they were God's people and that one day he would send them a Deliverer or Messiah. As we look briefly at the lives of four of their national heroes, we see that religion for the Israelites was not merely a by-product of life; it was life itself – their one purpose for living.

The first is Abraham, the 'Father of the Jewish race'. Nearly four thousand years ago he was born and brought up a pagan in the city of Ur, which lay half-way between Baghdad and the Persian Gulf. In later life, with his father, family, and servants, he left this great city of nearly a quarter of a million inhabitants and became a nomad. It was then that he made the great discovery that for him there was but one God, Jehovah (or perhaps more correctly 'Yahweh'). Other religions were dominated by fear, superstition, and cruelty, but Abraham learnt that his God hated human sacrifice and expected, not fear, but trust and devotion. With this remarkable faith he trekked six hundred miles into Canaan and there set up altars to Yahweh and by his fine example taught his people the goodness of God. This new faith marks for the Jews the beginning of their history.

Seven hundred years later we find the same faith in Moses. The Israelites were now slaves in Egypt, and Pharaoh denied them the right to worship God in their own way. Moses, who by accident had been brought up in Pharaoh's palace, knew how to talk to kings and princesses. He argued with Pharaoh. As a result, on that famous night of the first Passover, he led the Israelites out of slavery. Later, in the wilderness, he presented them with the Ten Commandments as from God, and all the laws he laid down for them assumed that God and not Moses was the real ruler of the nation. Through all the long years in which he moulded them into a civilised nation he claimed to be nothing more than God's mouthpiece.

A few generations later we find the Israelites in Palestine, governed by their most brilliant leader, David. As a boy facing the giant Goliath he declared, 'You come to me with a sword and with a spear and with a javelin, but I come to you in the name of the Lord of Hosts.' And through his life the same faith, common to Abraham and Moses, dominated his outlook. A brilliant general, statesman, administrator, poet, and musician, he composed some of the most beautiful psalms sung in Jewish synagogues and Christian churches today.

Finally, we have the warrior Judas Maccabeus, who symbolises the Jews as they so often appear in history – a small nation fighting against almost hopeless odds to keep their religion. In the second century B.C.E. they were suffering under the tyranny of an ex-general of Alexander the Great's army. He forbade the Jews to practice their religion, insisting that they should worship the Greek god Zeus. In the tremendous struggle that followed, Judas Maccabeus led the rebel Jews to victory. At first they were a small ill-armed band of men hunted in the Judean hills. Judas saw his father and two brothers perish in the struggle, but he held on and with great courage trained an army of outlaws which eventually cast the tyrant out of the country and made the Jews independent again for many years.

Of course, there were always some Jews who lost faith, and

83

even kings, at times, who lacked this brilliant vision of God's leadership. They turned to idol worship or made a pretence of goodness by offering many sacrifices instead of doing the will of God. When this happened a 'prophet' always appeared in Israel. A prophet is someone who is usually thought of as foretelling the future. But the prophets of Israel were not fortune-tellers. Far from it. They were the conscience of the nation; men like Elijah, Isaiah, and Jeremiah, called by God to save his people from disaster. Often they were men of humble life, herdsmen or vine-dressers, whose only claim to speak was that God inspired them. Their prophecies usually began with the words, 'Thus saith the Lord'. They showed great courage in facing angry rulers and people who did not want their own greed, vanity, or idolatry to be exposed. Jeremiah, for example, was thrown into a pit and left to starve because in his great patriotism and faith in God he denounced the government of his day.

Many of the prophets' writings have been preserved in the Jewish Scriptures. We cannot read them even today without being impressed by the living faith in God which they reveal.

### Eighteen centuries of persecution

Without this faith it seems hardly possible that the Jews could have survived, as a nation, the miserable fate that lay before them at the beginning of the Christian era. Few people nowadays realise that the Nazi massacre of six million Jews was just another episode on the long road of suffering that the Jews have travelled.

Under the harsh rule of the Romans the Jews sought their independence first in C.E. 66 and again in C.E. 132. After each insurrection the Romans treated them with terrible cruelty, massacring some and deporting others into slavery. Finally, a temple to Jupiter was built in place of the Jewish Temple which was burnt down, and the Jews were forbidden ever to return to Jerusalem. From that time until the twentieth century they ceased to have a homeland, living as best they could among foreigners.

After the fall of the Roman Empire the leaders of the Christian Church gradually built order out of chaos. Their main concern with the Jews was that they should be converted to Christianity; otherwise, as Jews, they were denied civic rights, required to pay the heaviest of taxes, and forbidden to convert others to Judaism.

When in the seventh century a new religion, Islam, appeared, its founder, Muhammad, first tried to win the Jews to his teaching. When he failed he killed many of them and sold others into slavery. For two centuries during the violent expansion of the Muslim Empire the Jews suffered. Only under the Moors in Spain during the ninth and tenth centuries did they live safely and in prosperity.

In 1290 they were expelled from England to the cries of howling mobs, and not until Cromwell's day were they generally readmitted. Between 1348 and 1350 the whole Jewish population in Germany was wiped out. In 1492 they were expelled from Spain. Eighty thousand managed to gain entry into Portugal on paying a large sum of money, but in 1495 they too were expelled.

So the wretched story continues – the greatest example in history of 'man's inhumanity to man'. The Jews were tortured by the Inquisition, burnt alive for supposedly causing plagues, and during the Crusades it was said that to kill a Jew would save a Christian from purgatory.

After the Renaissance, conditions began to improve slightly. But it was not until the eighteenth century, the Age of Reason, when men began to lay aside their blind prejudices and seek a reasonable basis for their beliefs and actions, that the Jews were looked upon as fellow human beings. Equal rights with other men were still, however, a distant goal. For example, it was not until 1858 in England that a Jew was allowed to sit in the House of Commons, and 1871 before he was permitted to take a degree at Oxford or Cambridge.

## The causes of anti-Semitism

Why were the Jews persecuted in this way? A complete answer would be impossible, so much depending upon local conditions in each period of history. No doubt the refusal of the Jews to give up their religion irritated their rulers. They were nearly always a subject race and were expected to conform to religious as well as political systems. Further, since the birth of Christianity, the fact that their ancestors were responsible for the death of Christ has been on occasion used against them. Then persecution itself made them a race apart. They were forbidden to introduce their religion to other people, and, thus driven in upon themselves, they were increasingly misunderstood and their religious practices became secret and open to suspicion. Absurd rumours were spread about: that, for instance, they killed Christian children in order to obtain blood for unleavened bread. Again, because they were disliked, they were prohibited by the medieval guilds from taking part in crafts and commerce. Thus many of them became moneylenders, a very unpopular occupation.

Whatever conclusions may be reached on this question, most civilised people today feel that anti-Semitism has been an unhappy and disgraceful chapter in the history of humanity, and that the sooner it is finally closed, the better.

# Judaism

## 12. *Torah* and *Talmud*

Genesis, Exodus, Leviticus, Numbers, Deuteronomy: these are the most important books in the Jewish Scriptures. Together they are called the Law, or the *Torah*. They describe how God selected the Hebrews to be his Chosen People and the promises he made to them, first through Abraham and then through Moses. The *Torah* also records the laws which the Hebrews and their descendants must keep if God is to fulfil these promises. This book is considered so sacred that no other book is ever allowed to be placed on top of it, and when a new copy is required, it is written with infinite care on special parchment.

Much later in the history of the Jews another book also appeared, the *Talmud*. Like many sacred books it began orally and was at first simply an interpretation of the *Torah* by famous teachers, known as Pharisees. As the centuries, passed, however, its scope was widened until it became a vast encyclopedia of Jewish thought and experience, including not only faith and morals but medicine, biology, science, and astronomy. In the sixth and seventh centuries C.E. it was written down and has remained a source of strength and unity to the Jewish nation ever since. It might well be called the official guide-book to the Jewish religion.

From these two sources, then, the *Torah* and the *Talmud*, can be gathered the general teaching of Judaism, and we shall consider now some of its main beliefs and customs.

### God, man, and his neighbour

As we have already seen, the belief in one God is the foundation of the Jewish faith. He alone created the universe and sustains it from hour to hour. Otherwise it would dissolve into nothing. On no account must any likeness of God appear anywhere. 'Thou shalt not make unto thyself any graven image,' declares the Second Commandment. Thus in the Jewish synagogue there are no statues or pictures or any other objects that might be taken to represent God. This prohibition was intended from the beginning to guard the Jew against the temptation to idolatry.

Since God is good, his people also must be good. There is no substitute for the good life. 'What does the Lord require of thee,' says the prophet Micah, 'but to do justice and to love mercy and to walk humbly with thy God.' The *Talmud* insists that without morality there can be no true religion. It even goes so far as to say, 'The heathen who observes the moral law is the equal of the High Priest.'

The Ten Commandments emphasise the negative side of this law. 'Thou shalt not kill, commit adultery, steal, bear false witness or covet.' But even these commandments, if they were kept, would make the world a much happier and safer place in which to live. Elsewhere in the *Torah* we get the positive side of man's duty to his neighbour. Every man has a right to live, to work, to have food and shelter, to hold possessions, and to have leisure and freedom. The employer must pay a fair wage and the employee give a fair return for it. The treatment of one's enemies, whether Jew or Gentile, must be merciful. 'If thine enemy be hungry, give him bread; if he be thirsty, give him water.' Kindness should extend even to the lower animals, which, if sick, should be cared for with the consideration given to human beings. In the Ten Commandments it is stressed that not only man but his domestic animals shall enjoy the rest and freedom of the sabbath day.

The special relationship between God and his people also carries a special responsibility. By their example the Jews must bring other nations to see God in his true character and to join them in worshipping and serving him.

## The future life

Judaism teaches that the Kingdom of God will come upon this earth. A Messiah, a mortal leader, the *Talmud* declares, will lead the Jews back to their homeland, and peace, happiness, and prosperity will radiate from the Jewish nation throughout mankind. It is pointed out that Jesus of Nazareth could never be accepted as Messiah because he did not fulfil this role. He was 'a Man of Sorrows', and through him much suffering has come to the Jewish people. The traditional view is simply expressed in the words of Maimonides, the great Jewish philosopher. 'All the prophets declare that the Messiah will be the deliverer of Israel and their saviour. But he caused Israel to perish by the sword, their remnant to be dispersed and humbled. He induced them to change the *Torah* and led the greater part of the world to err and to serve another beside God.' The true Messiah, however, will radiate happiness, bringing joy and freedom to his Chosen People and establish God's Kingdom on earth in preparation for his eternal Kingdom in heaven.

Finally, there will be a general resurrection of the dead and a Day of Judgement. The wicked will be punished, but not for ever. The good will enter a new life of spiritual development and increasing prosperity.

Gentiles will not be excluded from this future life. Those in every age who lived the good life and acknowledged God as sovereign of the world will enter his eternal Kingdom.

## The practice of religion

Both the *Torah* and the *Talmud* give directions for the personal practice of the Jewish faith. Of course, many of the regulations in the *Torah* refer to conditions of life in the desert of Sinai and later in Palestine. Nevertheless, some of them were well in advance of their time. If, for instance, the laws of sanitation as laid down in the *Torah* had been observed in the Middle Ages, it is unlikely that plagues such as the Black

Death would have swept across Europe and certainly the stench and filth of our medieval towns would never have been tolerated. Though regulations such as these are now out of date, many others, especially those relating to the devotional life, are still carried out.

In private life the two most important factors for the Jewish family are the home and the synagogue. On the doorpost of many Jewish homes there is a small metal cylinder or box called a *mezuzah*. It contains a text from the *Torah* inscribed on a minute scroll. As a Jew enters the house he will touch the *mezuzah* with his fingers and in doing so acknowledge that a Jewish home is also a holy place. In it he will be constantly reminded of his faith.

Regular and frequent prayer is a part of his daily life. Immediately on rising in the morning he washes his hands and offers a prayer of thanksgiving for the new day. Washing of the hands also precedes the eating of food at any time, and prayers are said both before and after meals. Other prayers are offered during the day and in the evening. Special prayers mark the beginning of the sabbath on Friday evenings, when candles are lit and a short service is conducted round the supper table. Prayers are provided also for unusual occasions: the receiving of good news, the buying of a house or new clothes, meeting distinguished or inspiring people, and always on occasions of danger and distress.

Family life is all-important. Gentiles sometimes refer to a bachelor as living in 'the state of single blessedness'. But the *Talmud* declares, 'He who has no wife lives without happiness, without religion and without blessing.' All marriages are religious ceremonies, and, although divorce and remarriage are allowed by Jewish law, the Jews set a good example to the rest of the world by their deep respect for married life. It is a sacred duty to bring up children in the Jewish faith. Boys are circumcised on the eighth day after birth, an act performed by either a doctor or a registered circumciser.

At this important ceremony a baby is given his Hebrew

name which is used henceforth on all official occasions. One of these is his Bar-Mitzvah. On the sabbath following his thirteenth birthday, he reads a passage from the *Torah* in Hebrew before the congregation. This marks his coming of age and he can then be counted as one of the ten male adults necessary for the holding of a synagogue service. The Bar-Mitzvah is usually marked by a great family celebration. Girls come of age at twelve and this may be followed by a ceremony in the synagogue.

In many Jewish homes great care is taken over food, as the dietary laws based on the *Torah* are still observed. Jews may not eat certain animals and fish, especially shellfish. Milk and meat must never be served together. Most people know the importance of 'kosher' to the Jews. The word refers to the selection, slaughter, and preparation of animals for food. Only when the regulations have been carried out to the satisfaction of the local rabbi is the food acceptable to the orthodox Jew. These ancient regulations probably first appeared in the interests of health; they are kept today mainly as an exercise in self-discipline, and, of course, as a require-ment of the *Torah*.

The Jewish character of the home is therefore very import-ant. This is the wife's domain. She is responsible for making sure that the laws regarding food are observed, that proper arrangements are made for festivals and other special occasions. Above all she has the care and instruction of her children to attend to until, at the age of five, they begin special classes in the Jewish faith. She may, of course, go out to work, provided the home and children do not suffer in any way. But in recent years liberal-minded Jews have taken a less rigid view of a woman's responsibility in the home, and women have, in fact, become rabbis.

### The synagogue

Long before the Christian Church appeared, when the only serious rival was the pagan temple, the Jewish synagogues bore solitary witness to an unwavering faith in God. In the twentieth century they continue virtually the same as they were then. Little in their appearance attracts attention, for neither inside nor out do they attempt to compete with the wealthy and ornate buildings of other religions. The interior strikes a non-Jew as bare. The centre of reverence is the Ark of the Covenant, a recess or cupboard, in front of which a small lamp burns perpetually. In the Ark are kept the Scrolls of the Law. They are covered with beautifully embroidered cloth, and before the Ark hangs a rich curtain. The Ark is always at the east end of the synagogue so that the congregation in facing it are themselves turned towards Jerusalem throughout their worship. Men and women usually sit separately, the women in a gallery. The men must keep their heads covered inside the synagogue and the women must do so at least on the sabbath. The service is conducted from a raised platform from which the *Torah* is read, and the readings are so arranged that the whole of the Law is heard in the course of a year. The principal officer of the synagogue, not priest, is a rabbi, assisted by a leader who recites prayers and a cantor who leads the singing. During the service a scroll of the *Torah* is taken from the Ark and carried round the synagogue. Everybody present turns towards it and either bows or touches it as a mark of deep reverence.

Services are held frequently in the synagogue, but the day of greatest activity is the sabbath, which begins at sunset on Friday and 'dies' about sunset on Saturday. During these twenty-four hours Jews do as little work as possible. Very strict Jews will not travel on the sabbath; some will not even use a telephone. Other occasions of great religious activity are the festivals during the year, of which the following are the most important.

The Jewish New Year (Rosh Hashanah) is celebrated in September or October. It is a reminder of God's creation of the world. In the synagogue a ram's horn is blown to recall the people of God. Good wishes for the new year are

...ced that the first five books of the Old Testament
...ot written by Moses at all, but centuries after he had
...oday we know that some of this early criticism was
...e and ill-considered, but few people realised this at the
...he results were serious: many Jews lost their faith
...er; others clung to their belief in God and his special
...nce for the Jewish race, while they began to give up
...ious customs and traditions based on the *Torah*.

## ...t of assimilation on Judaism

...ile Jewish communities everywhere were learning to
...rmony with the Gentile nations. They felt that they
...ve their loyalty to their adopted countries by con-
...to their way of life. Remarkable changes occurred.
...ws refused to consider themselves any longer as a
...ation: they were merely a sect with certain religious
...ynagogue services were altered to conform with the
...f Christian worship. Hebrew gave place to the
...of the country; Sunday was adopted as the day of
...d of Saturday; men and women sat together in the
...; their children were 'confirmed' at Whitsuntide.
...other hand, many Jews were scandalized by these
...' tendencies. The only hope for the race, they felt,
...a deaf ear to all modern criticism and maintain
...ancient customs and beliefs of their faith. Such
...ay are known as Orthodox Jews. They accept the
...ich should be studied daily, as the supreme
...ts laws especially in relation to the sabbath and to
...be rigidly observed. Prayers should be said three
...; children given regular instruction in the faith;
...rabbi treated with the highest respect. Orthodox
...not accept women as rabbis. They believe that
...l come to restore Israel to her rightful place
...ations and eventually draw all men unto him.
...be expected, a middle party eventually arose.
...irm for the Jewish way of life and kept an open

exchanged and apples dipped in honey are eaten.

The Day of Atonement (Yom Kippur), is the last day of ten days' penitence following the New Year. It is a day of prayer, confession and repentance. A devout Jew may fast for 24 hours and spend most of his time in the synagogue. The day recalls the one occasion in the year when the High Priest used to enter the Holy of Holies and also make prayer and sacrifice for the people.

The Feast of Tabernacles (Sukkot) follows five days later. It is a reminder of God's care for the Israelites in the wilderness of Sinai. The synagogue is decorated with fruit and flowers; shelters (tabernacles) made of branches are erected in gardens or near the synagogue and meals taken there during the following week.

The Festival of Lights (Hannukah) is a joyful occasion about the time of Christmas in the Christian calendar. It is in memory of the great victory of Judas Maccabeus and the rededication of the Temple in 164 B.C.E. The festival lasts eight days and each day a fresh candle is lit, children receive presents and games are often played.

The Passover or the Feast of Unleavened Bread (Pesach) takes place around the time of the Christian Easter. At home on the eve of the Passover, the youngest child asks the question 'Why is this night different from all other nights?' Then his father explains how it recalls a night 3,000 years ago when their ancestors were slaves in Egypt and during the hours of darkness the Angel of Death smote the Egyptians and Moses led the Israelites out into the desert. During the Passover meal (Seder) and for the next eight days the family eats Matzos, unleavened bread, reminding them of the exodus, and a nut and apple paste to remind them of the mortar which they used to make bricks for the Egyptians.

Pentecost or the Feast of Weeks (Shavuot) follows fifty days of mourning after Passover. It recalls the failure of the Jewish revolt against Rome in the second century and it also commemorates Moses receiving the Law from God. The

synagogue is decorated and the Ten Commandments are read to the congregation.

Though, as we see from this brief survey, religion is a vital part of everyday life for the Jews, they do not seek to convert others to Judaism. They believe that since their daughter religions, Christianity and Islam, are missionary religions and contain so much of the essential truth, missionary work can be left to them. The Jews are very tolerant. Their rule for many centuries has been that of the prophet Micah, 'Let all others adhere to their creed and worship and let us walk in the name of our God for ever.'

# Judaism

## 13. Modern developm

Freedom from persecution char
pletely. No longer were the Jev
nor had they to be ready, at a
their lives. Instead, they wer
problem: could they make a s
friendship with their fellow
some of them to prove that th
helpful to the state that they
religious faith and practice
religion. But while they were
changes, their religion itself
who had begun to study the
Criticism.

### Source Criticism and Judais

By considering the histori
discover the source of th
example, by this method
Isaiah consists in fact c
different periods by at le

How did this criticis
moment the most impor

'I believe with perfect
possession, is the sam
peace be unto him.'

This belief has been
doubt a syllable of the 7
it had come, word for v
Imagine, then, how

annou
were
died.
extren
time.
altoget
provid
the rel

*The effe*
Meanw
live in h
must pr
forming
Many J
separate
beliefs.
pattern
language
rest inste
synagogu

On the
'modernis
was to tu
rigidly the
people to
*Torah*, w
authority.
diet shoul
times a da
and the loc
Jews woul
Messiah w
among the

As migh
They stood

mind about Bible criticism. Nevertheless, they felt that the time had come to modify some of their ancient customs. So we have today Liberal or Reformed Jews, and in their synagogues we may find stained-glass windows, an organ and choir, and families sitting together. Their beliefs, too, have altered. The coming of Messiah is no longer important; the teaching of the Prophets is given more weight than the Law; and some Liberal Jews are quite prepared to study the life of Jesus, recognizing him to be the greatest moral teacher that their race has produced. But the vast majority of Jews remain orthodox, though they do make some concessions to the conditions of the twentieth century.

It is wise to keep an open mind on Bible criticism. Such criticism is rarely final, especially as the critics themselves often differ in opinion. Moreover, in recent years Jewish scholars have answered much of the early criticism which so distressed the Jewish people. Just as one may follow the varying theories of scientists about the origin of the world and man without one's faith in God being seriously affected, so one may follow the investigations of the Higher Critics without doubting that the Bible will remain God's revelation of himself through man. After all, the most important question is not whether Moses wrote the *Torah* but whether God inspired it.

### Zionism

Out of these generally disturbing conditions arose a movement known as Zionism. Zion is another name for Jerusalem, and Zionism was the name given to the urge among Jews of all nations to return to Palestine and to found another Jewish state there.

The movement has grown rapidly in the last sixty years. In the first place, the conception of a worldwide 'Return to Palestine' is a deeply religious one, prayed for and believed in through all the centuries of persecution. In a dark world it was the one inspiration that gave the Jews any hope at all.

Also, in recent years Zionism has flourished for a very different reason. As we have seen, many Jews, when persecution ceased, began to compromise in their faith and practice in deference to Gentile rulers for leaving them in peace. Their own leaders became alarmed lest the race should disappear altogether. They argued that the only way to save their people would be through the establishment of a new Jewish state where they could live uninfluenced by their Gentile neighbours. Finally, a third incentive to Zionism was the fact that the Jews in some countries still continued to suffer. In Russia, as late as 1882, the Tsar made drastic laws against them, and later, in France, anti-Jewish riots occurred. Was anti-Semitism, after all, an incurable disease? If so, Zionism was the only answer. So the first Zionist Conference took place in 1897. As a consequence, small farming settlements began to appear in Palestine. They prospered indifferently until, twenty years later, the famous Balfour Declaration acknowledged the claim of the Jews to Palestine, and pledged the British government to support the establishment of a Jewish National Home there.

Britain was uniquely involved in this new venture because in the same year her army had driven the Turks out of Palestine (and virtually out of the First World War) and she became responsible for the state of the country, establishing first a military and then a civil administration. Later she accepted a mandate for the territory from the League of Nations. It proved a thankless task.

The League had welcomed the Balfour Declaration and between 1920 and 1929 300,000 Jewish immigrants arrived, bought land from the Arabs and made it quite clear that they intended to establish in Palestine a Jewish state. This infuriated the vast majority of the Arab population, who saw themselves being slowly dispossessed of the country they had inhabited for over a thousand years. Between 1929 and 1938 there were four Arab rebellions. A commission in 1937 recommended partition of the country into separate Arab and

Jewish states, but neither side would agree to the terms.

The situation worsened with the immigration pressure caused by the holocaust in Germany under Hitler. The British found themselves between two fires: the clamour by Jewish refugees to enter Palestine and the bitter efforts of the Arabs to keep them out. Under this pressure Britain in 1939 limited immigrants to a final 75,000. The tension eased a little during the Second World War when both Jews and Arabs fought voluntarily on the side of the Allies but when peace was resumed there followed widespread outrages by Jewish terrorists. Britain appealed for a solution to the United Nations who proposed another partition which again was not accepted. So Britain finally decided in 1948 to surrender her mandate and the Jewish Agency responsible for the settlements immediately proclaimed an independent State of Israel.

Since then, Israel has maintained her independence by force of arms largely supplied from abroad. For many years it has been a hard and bitter struggle and will remain so as long as Israel meets with hostility from her neighbours.

The majority of Jews remain outside Palestine. Some who are not Zionists believe that they have no right to forsake the country of their birth which has nurtured, educated and protected them. Others argue that the state of Israel is manmade and is not the fulfilment of ancient prophecy which declared that God himself will lead his people to the Promised Land. Until then the Jews must wait and not contrive things for themselves.

Within the state of Israel, however, the ancient customs of her people are strictly observed. Hebrew is the national language taught in all their schools; Saturday is the national day of rest when all work is reduced to a minimum, shops are shut and trains do not run; and law and customs are based on *Torah* and *Talmud*. And the belief is still held by many that in his own time God, through his Chosen People, will bring together all the family of mankind in peace and righteousness.

99

# From the Jewish Scriptures

And God spoke all these words saying, 'I am the Lord your God: you shall have no other gods before me.

'You shall not make yourself a graven image, or any likeness of anything that is in heaven above, or that is in the earth beneath, or that is in the water under the earth. You shall not bow down to them or serve them.

'You shall not take the name of the Lord your God in vain.
'Remember the sabbath day, to keep it holy.
'Honour your father and your mother.
'You shall not kill.
'You shall not commit adultery.
'You shall not steal.
'You shall not bear false witness against your neighbour.
'You shall not covet.'

(Exodus 20:1)

The Lord is my shepherd, I shall not want; he makes me lie down in green pastures. He leads me beside still waters; he restores my soul. He leads me in paths of righteousness for His name's sake. Even though I walk through the valley of the shadow of death, I fear no evil; for thou art with me; thy rod and thy staff, they comfort me.

(Psalm 23)

What does the Lord require of you but to do justice, and to love kindness, and to walk humbly with your God?

(Micah 6:8)

1. An Australian bushman pointing his magic stick at the man he wishes to kill.

2. Monkeys in this temple in Benares are treated with religious veneration in honour of the monkey god, Hanuman, and are allowed to roam about at will.

**3.** An ancient temple to Shiva in Madras. Built in the sixth century, it was one of seven, the others having since been washed into the sea.

4. For many hours this young Hindu has stood half submerged in the sacred waters of the Ganges in religious meditation.

5. Mahatma Gandhi photographed in England with the 'Red' Dean of Canterbury, Dr Hewlett Johnson, in 1931.

**6.** The Buddhist Temple in Bihar, built on the site
of the pipal tree where Gautama received his enlightenment.

7. Buddhist monks receiving food.

8. Kuan-yin, the bodhisattva of whom the Dalai Lama of Tibet is believed to be the reincarnation.

**9.** An N.C.O. in the Thai army in meditation before a statue of the Buddha covered with gold leaf. Before he leaves the soldier will stick the piece of gold leaf he holds between his fingers on the statue.

**10.** A figure of the Buddha with a golden halo, in Nara, Japan. It is the largest bronze statue in the world: 452 tons.

**11.** The Dalai Lama of Tibet being greeted by the Archbishop of Canterbury in Lambeth Palace, 1981.

**12.** A statue to Confucius in Taischung on the island of Formosa, where many people still study and follow his teaching.

**13.** Celebrating New Year's Day in Tokyo. Thousands of Japanese
visit the Meiji Shrine to pray for peace and prosperity in the New Year.

**14.** After marriage at the Shinto Shrine,
the bride and bridegroom return home for the wedding reception.

**15.** Pope John Paul II blesses a child as he arrives at Coventry Airport in May 1982.

**16.** A synagogue service. The consecration of a synagogue rebuilt
after the Second World War in Worms. The Mayor of Worms is speaking.

**17.** A kibbutz (settlement) in Galilee, one of many in Israel where Jews
have worked under rigorous conditions to reclaim and farm the land.

**18.** The remains of the synagogue in Capernaum which is believed to be the one built by the centurion whose servant Jesus healed.

**19.** A Christian congregation at Brentwood Cathedral.

20. The Sanctuary Knocker at the Church of St Nicholas, Gloucester. It represents the devil carrying off a fugitive whose tongue is lolling out with exhaustion and trying to reach the grape vine above.

21. The Archbishop of Canterbury in procession at Canterbury Cathedral.

**22.** The *Ka'aba* in Mecca, the holiest shrine in Islam. Its gold-embroidered covering is renewed annually by the Egyptian government. The keeper shown here claims that his ancestors have looked after the shrine for six hundred years.

**23.** Muslims in Kenya at prayer.

**24.** The sixteenth-century Edirne mosque,
considered to be the most beautiful one in Turkey.

25. Sikhs worshipping in their great temple in Delhi.

**26.** Queue outside the entrance to Lenin's tomb in the Kremlin, Moscow.

They shall beat their swords into ploughshares, and their spears into pruning hooks; nation shall not lift up sword against nation, neither shall they learn war any more.

(Isaiah 2 : 4)

Have you not known? Have you not heard? The Lord is the everlasting God, the Creator of the ends of the earth. He does not faint or grow weary, his understanding is unsearchable. He gives power to the faint, and to him who has no might he increases strength. Even youths shall faint and be weary, and young men shall fall exhausted; but they who wait for the Lord shall renew their strength, they shall mount up with wings like eagles, they shall run and not be weary, they shall walk and not faint.

(Isaiah 40 : 28)

# Points for discussion

1 What do you think are the main reasons for anti-Semitism? How can Gentiles and Jews help to overcome it?

2 In what ways do you think the Jews have shown themselves to be a 'Chosen People'?

3 What is Zionism? Find out all you can about the new State of Israel. Do you think that this can be a successful experiment?

4 'The house is the wife's domain.' This traditional view is sometimes questioned today. Do you think that a wife should have the major authority and responsibility in the running of the home?

5 The Jews, despite persecution, have produced men of genius in every age. What Jews in modern times have distinguished themselves in the arts and in science? Find out what you can about them.

# Christianity

## 14. The life of Christ

Jesus, the founder of the Christian religion, was born in Palestine, a province of the Roman Empire, nearly two thousand years ago. The exact date is uncertain. The Roman monk who, in the sixth century, was the first to calculate it made a mistake of at least six years. So the date of Jesus's birth was 6 B.C. or a little earlier.

Though Jesus is mentioned by Josephus, the Jewish historian, and by two famous Romans, Tacitus and Pliny the Younger, our main information about him comes from the New Testament. Here we have four short books, known as gospels, recounting parts of his life. The first three, Matthew, Mark, and Luke, give very similar accounts; the fourth, John, is different in many ways and adds much to our knowledge of him.

### His early life

Jesus was born in a cattle-shed. A carpenter, Joseph, and his wife, Mary, happened to go from Nazareth to Bethlehem at this time for a census of the Jewish people. The town was overcrowded, and, as there was no room for them in the inn, Jesus was born during the night in a shed or cave. Matthew and Luke tell us that Mary was his mother and the Holy Spirit, his father. Luke also tells us that shepherds visited him on the night of his birth, and Matthew describes how some Eastern astrologers arrived a few weeks later bringing him gifts.

From Bethlehem the family fled to Egypt out of the reach of Herod the Great, ruler of Palestine. He had heard from the astrologers about the birth of a king in Bethlehem and he plotted to kill Jesus as a possible rival. After about two years, following the death of Herod, the family returned to Palestine and settled in Nazareth again.

We have no further news of Jesus for over thirty years, except for one episode. At twelve years of age, with Mary and Joseph, he visited Jerusalem. There for a time he was lost, only to be found later disputing expertly with the lawyers in the Temple.

Then suddenly after thirty years a remarkable event took place. There appeared near the River Jordan a hermit called John, who declared that God was about to send his long-expected Messiah (Deliverer) to the Jewish nation. 'Repent,' he cried, 'for the Kingdom of God is at hand.' The Jews, greatly disturbed, were baptized in hundreds in the Jordan to signify their repentance. Only the religious leaders stood aloof because they felt that John did not treat them with proper respect. Jesus himself came. As he stepped out of the water he heard a voice say, 'This is my beloved son in whom I am well pleased. He knew then that he must begin his work, so he retired to a neighbouring desert to prepare for it in solitude.

## The Condition of Palestine

Had we lived in Jerusalem about this time we should probably have been astonished at the number of people who claimed some sort of authority either to issue orders or to give advice. First there was Pontius Pilate, the governor of Judea. He held his post from Caesar, and, provided that he kept order and made sure that Rome profited financially from her little province, his position was fairly secure. Then there were the Roman soldiers always about the streets, demanding the respect and obedience of the inhabitants. A lesser breed, though nevertheless quite powerful, were the tax-collectors who made sure that the Jews paid handsomely for the Roman occupation. With few exceptions they were grossly dishonest and very rich. In addition, on the side of the government were the Sadducees, a party mainly composed of wealthy priests. With the High Priest as leader they were responsible for the Temple sacrifices and were content to advise everyone to obey the Romans and keep the peace.

Most of the Jews, however, hated the Romans and prayed for the Messiah to come to destroy them. An extreme party were the Zealots, who saw no reason even to wait for the Messiah. Had not their hero, Judas Maccabeus, freed Palestine only two centuries ago from a worse tyrant than Rome? From their hide-outs in the Judean hills they carried on a ceaseless guerrilla warfare against the Romans.

There were still three more groups of people: Scribes, Pharisees, and Essenes. They all counselled a lofty indifference to Rome. The Scribes interpreted the Jewish Law, which had become so cumbersome that there were 613 commandments to be observed. The Pharisees tried to keep the Law because they believed that it was the only means of salvation. Many of them were hard-working teachers, but most of them had grown contemptuous of the common people, especially those who behaved badly. They were very intolerant too. At this period they were even refusing to sit on the same council (Sanhedrin) with the Sadducees. Finally, there were the Essenes, whom Josephus said were to be found in every town. They considered themselves 'the Saints of God, the Children of Light', living in the last days before the overthrow of the Kingdom of Satan. Some traces of an Essene community have been recently unearthed near the Dead Sea, and the famous Scrolls contain relics of their beliefs and their commentaries on the books of the Old Testament.

Faced with this explosive situation in Palestine, Jesus was sorely tempted to use the great powers he felt within him to become a popular Messiah. During his forty days in solitude he seems to have battled with two main temptations: to win the people over to him by magic and to turn out the Romans by force. In the end he resisted both of them; his victories were to be won by other means.

## The period of popularity

He chose as his centre for work Capernaum, a town on the shores of the Sea of Galilee. This was a busy place with a Roman garrison, a customs house, and much business in agriculture and fishing.

He became immediately popular. To assist him he chose twelve disciples, later known as the Apostles. His popularity stemmed first from his miracles. Wherever he went, even outside his own country, he was anxious to relieve suffering. Certain 'nature miracles' are also attributed to him, such as stilling a storm at sea, turning water into wine, and feeding five thousand people with five loaves and two fishes. It is recorded that he brought three people back to life: the daughter of a synagogue official, Jairus; the son of a widow from the town of Nain; and Lazarus, the brother of two close friends living in Bethany. But most of all he concerned himself with mental and bodily diseases, which he eagerly cured out of pity for the sufferers.

Another feature that made him popular was his superb method of teaching. His language was simple and pleasing to the ear, for when it is translated back into his native tongue we discover that it reveals the qualities of fine poetry. He had a genius for storytelling and rarely failed to entertain his audience with a parable that contained a hidden meaning. He spoke with an air of absolute authority so that men were deeply moved by his words and often felt that they were listening to the voice of God himself.

Finally, it is clear that his very company was a delight to those who met him. He loved ordinary people, was happily entertained in their homes, attended their weddings, blessed their children, enjoyed their feasts, and gladly relieved their sufferings. He brought happiness and a new hope to men who found life dreary and hopeless under the Roman yoke. So people tramped miles to hear him, climbed trees to catch a glimpse of him, gave him hardly time to eat or pray, and at least once plotted to carry him off and proclaim him king.

## Decline and death

There were two occasions when it is recorded that Jesus wept: over the death of his friend, Lazarus, and over Jerusalem, because he could not save it. This latter incident gives us a clue to the tragedy that finally overtook him. While the common people heard him gladly, their leaders rejected him, and Jesus knew that sooner or later they would again dominate the life of the nation and that the state of Israel would be just as if he had never lived. Lawyers, Pharisees, and Sadducees came down from Jerusalem to listen to him and most of them denounced him as they had denounced the hermit John. He was too critical of the uselessness of their religion and the selfishness of their ideals. They said that he was blasphemous because he forgave sins, that he was a winebibber because he ate with outcasts, and that he performed his miracles by the power of the devil. Tension mounted between them, and Jesus knew that there was only one course open to him.

And so it came about that on one of those occasions when Jesus retired into the country to teach his disciples, he asked them bluntly who they thought he was. Peter, their spokesman, replied, 'Thou art the Christ, the Son of the Living God.' Having thus made quite sure of their faith in him, he proceeded to tell them that, as Christ (Messiah), he was about to suffer a cruel and humiliating death. They were aghast: surely Messiah was going to be victorious! But despite their arguments and stubborn opposition he set out for Jerusalem, the centre of hostility.

Once there, it seems that he acted with the intention of bringing matters swiftly to a head. As Messiah, he rode on a donkey – a symbol of humility – into Jerusalem and made for the Temple. There the parables he told implied that he was 'the Anointed One of God'. The real clash came on the following day. He defied the High Priest by clearing the

Temple courts of traders and money changers, scattering their goods and coins in all directions. 'It is written,' he thundered, 'My house shall be called a house of prayer, but you are making it a robbers' cave!' From that moment events moved swiftly. Judas, a disciple, compounded with the High Priest to lead the Temple soldiers to where they could arrest him. But Jesus was not yet ready.

With great secrecy he met his disciples by night in a room in Jerusalem for what is now called 'the Last Supper'. There he talked and prayed with them, washed their feet as a sign of humble service, and promised them the gift of the Holy Spirit. During supper he broke the bread and gave a piece to each of them, saying, 'This is my body'; and handing them also the wine he said, 'This is my blood. Do this in remembrance of me.'

A short while afterwards he was arrested on the slopes of the Mount of Olives. Faced with Temple soldiers and a mob armed with sticks, the disciples quickly slipped away. Jesus faced his trial and death alone.

There were two trials. The first was before the High Priest and the Jewish Council. After much bungling of evidence, the Council eventually condemned him for blasphemy. But since they could not carry out the death sentence they took him to the Governor, Pontius Pilate. Here again there was delay. Pilate, roused from his bed perhaps a little too early, was in no mood to talk religion either with the prisoner or with his accusers. He cared nothing for the charge of blasphemy, and on what other charge he could condemn Jesus he had no idea. Moreover, he seems to have been almost afraid of this silent and dignified stranger. 'Have nothing to do with that innocent man,' advised his wife when she heard who it was. But though Pilate hedged, the priests were determined. 'He calls himself a King. We have no King but Caesar. If you let this man go, you are no friend to Caesar!' This was dangerous talk, and so Pilate passed sentence on him. After both trials Jesus was buffeted, spat upon, and treated with all the ignominy and brutality a helpless man could suffer in a barrack-room in those days. He made no protest. Finally, crowned with a wreath of thorns, he dragged his cross the half-mile to the execution ground, Calvary, where for six hours from 9 a.m. to 3 p.m. he slowly died, forgiving his enemies as he did so.

## The Resurrection

There follows the most remarkable sequel to this tragic story. The body of Jesus was laid in the garden tomb of a friend, Joseph of Arimathea. The stone over the entrance was sealed and a Temple guard posted outside it. This happened on the Friday afternoon of his death. On the Sunday morning following, a few women went down to the grave to embalm the body. The tomb was empty.

Later, one of the women, Mary of Magdala, reported excitedly that she had met Jesus walking in the garden after the other women had left. The disciples dismissed the story as nonsense until they too actually met him. For forty days he appeared at various times. There are ten of these appearances recorded in the New Testament. Jesus assured his disciples that he was not a ghost; he invited them to touch him, and on one occasion sat down and, probably with a twinkle in his eye at their astonishment, ate a meal with them. Finally, before a great crowd, he ascended into heaven.

Unbelievable as these appearances seem to be, no one has ever been able to explain them away. All four gospels are definite about the fact that Jesus returned to life, though their accounts do not entirely agree. Moreover, something of this nature must have happened to explain the sudden revival of faith and courage in the disciples who were all but dead with grief and fear. Nor are men willing to suffer horrible martyrdom for something they are not positive is true. Paul wrote, 'If Christ be not risen, then is our preaching vain.' And it was this conviction that Jesus was alive that gave birth to the Christian religion.

# Christianity

## 15. The teaching of Christ

Though the teaching of Jesus is in simple language and often in story form, there are three reasons why it requires thoughtful study to understand it.

In the first place, it is not arranged in any convenient order. If we want to know what Jesus teaches on a particular subject, there may be half a dozen references to it in different parts of the gospels. Even if we write them down and study them, we may not fully understand their meaning unless we have also read the rest of his teaching. There is no complete statement of belief or easy set of rules for Christian conduct in the gospels. We can form only a general impression from our reading and think things out for ourselves.

Again, Jesus often exaggerated in order to make men think. Here are two examples. 'If anyone comes to me and does not hate his father and mother, wife and children, brothers and sisters, even his own life, he cannot be a disciple of mine'; and, 'You must not think that I have come to bring peace to the earth; I have not come to bring peace, but a sword.' Isolated quotations such as these can sometimes give a completely false idea of what Jesus is teaching. They are obviously not meant to be taken literally and yet they contain an important germ of truth.

Finally, the words Jesus uttered are only a part of his teaching. Of himself he said, 'Anyone who has seen me has seen the Father.' By this he meant that his actions were as important as his words. He intended that his whole life should be viewed as an object lesson, showing how God thinks, feels, and acts in his dealings with mankind.

Fortunately the gospels are short, for there is no real

substitute for reading them. A modern version, such as *The New English Bible*, may be very helpful. The following outline can give only a summary of some of the main points that Jesus made and about which he challenged men to think very seriously.

## The Reign of God

Jesus set out to teach men about 'the Kingdom of God' or 'the Kingdom of Heaven'. Perhaps the title 'the Reign of God' may be more helpful, since the subject has to do with men's minds rather than with kings, armies, and territory. He wished men to know that God could, in fact, reign over their lives if they would let him, since he was much more concerned about them than they imagined. His name for God was 'Father', though he acknowledged this to be inadequate, for the kindest of earthly fathers could never be as concerned about his family as God was about the human race. Jesus invited his audience to think about the care God lavished on his lesser creation, the flowers, the grass, and the birds. Not even a sparrow fell to the ground without his knowing about it. Jesus showed how much more valuable people were to God by telling such stories as 'the Parable of the Prodigal Son'.

He demonstrated this in his own life by deliberately seeking the company of the most despised people in society, such as the tax-collectors, who were condemned by everyone, and those who were ignored and forgotten because they were poor, diseased, or crippled. He was angry when his disciples suggested that mothers with their children were not important enough to take up his time. He tried to help everyone who came to him in real need. 'Come to me,' he said, 'all whose work is hard, whose load is heavy; and I will give you relief.' And finally he suffered the most degrading of deaths as a supreme act of love to save mankind.

Jesus was concerned when he found that so many people worried and fretted their way through life. If they would allow God to control their lives, their anxieties would change overnight to confidence and peace of mind.

This he maintained despite the evil in the world of which he was very conscious. He continually talked about it and summed it up in the person of the Devil or Satan, a malignant power, against whom his followers were bound to wage unceasing war. He spoke about natural calamities and made it clear that his followers must not expect to escape from them. Suffering was the lot of mankind. But his followers would know how to cope with it and even use it to advantage. His own death was an example of how a Christian could face suffering and emerge victorious.

Nevertheless, he seems to teach that suffering is not the will of God. It is a phase of our experience. Speaking of his healing he said, 'If it is by the finger of God that I drive out the devils, then be sure the Kingdom of God has already come upon you.' It is as if he were saying to those he healed, 'The joy and relief you and your friends are feeling now are typical of the Reign of God, and life will be like this for all men when the Reign of God comes everywhere.'

When would that be? Jesus definitely taught that at a certain point in time the life of mankind as we know it would end; there would be a solemn judgement, the wicked would be punished, those who had suffered wrongfully would be recompensed, and the future would be filled with the glory and the love of God. We do not know whether Jesus intended us to take this picture literally, but he made it clear that one day evil would be finally overthrown and God's reign would be universal. When that day would be he confessed that he did not know, but it would come suddenly and without warning. Meanwhile, earthly life was to be regarded as a challenging experience in preparation for an infinitely happier life that lay beyond space and time.

*What Jesus taught about himself*

Who was Jesus? This was the question continually on the lips of those who listened to him. People said he was a carpenter's son, but this they felt was not sufficient to explain his amazing power. Even his enemies admitted this. Nicodemus, a Pharisee, speaking for the Pharisees, said, 'We know that you are a teacher sent by God; no one could perform these signs of yours unless God were with him.' When soldiers were sent by the High Priest to arrest him, they returned empty-handed, exclaiming, 'No man ever spoke as this man speaks.' Was he a reincarnation of a great prophet of bygone days, Isaiah or Jeremiah? No one seemed to know.

Jesus called himself 'the Son of Man', but this did not answer their question, for no one properly understood what Jesus meant by this title. Even his disciples were mystified, and only from his acts and words, which implied that he was different from other men, did they finally decide that he was the Messiah.

He declared that he had the power to forgive sins, that he was Lord of the Sabbath, that his death would be 'a ransom for many', that he would return from the grave, and that at the end of time he would come back to judge all men. He said of himself, 'I am the light of the world'; 'No one comes to the Father except by me'; 'I am the bread of life'. On one occasion when he was talking to the Pharisees about Abraham, the founder of their race, they scoffed at him, saying, 'You are not yet fifty years old. How can you have seen Abraham?' He replied, 'Before Abraham was born, I am.' And on another occasion, talking to Martha as they approached the tomb of her brother, Lazarus, whom he raised from death, he said, 'I am the resurrection and I am life. If a man has faith in me, even though he die, he shall come to life; and no one who is alive and has faith shall ever die.'

Ordinary men do not speak in language like this, and there is no doubt that Jesus looked upon himself as unique. His closest friends gradually came to share this view. After the resurrection one of his disciples, Thomas, declared that he would not believe that Jesus was alive unless he could put his fingers into the wounds which had been made in Jesus's body. It is recorded that Jesus appeared to him and offered himself for the experiment. Thomas was overwhelmed, sank to his knees, and exclaimed, 'My Lord and my God.' These words actually summarize what all the disciples felt about him and what, in fact, they preached about him after he had left them.

## What Jesus taught about man

Jesus talked to everyone who would listen to him. He did not single out any class of men for his teaching, nor did he expect those who accepted it to forsake their usual way of life to become monks or hermits. This was a religion for the daily round and it was offered to everyone, whatever their race, colour, or rank. Early in his ministry he hoped that his own people, the Jews, would be the first to accept it, but when at the end he found this impossible, he said to his followers, 'Go forth to every part of the world and proclaim the Good News.'

In the eyes of Jesus man was more important to God than anything else in the universe. He alone was capable of knowing God as his father and accepting his friendship and guidance. Jesus himself set an example, and it was his life of faith and prayer that he wished everyone to discover for himself. Before, however, a man could realise this control of God in his life, there were two conditions to be fulfilled.

First, he must feel a real need for it. The self-satisfaction which so many of the Pharisees and Sadducees showed made their conversion impossible. And any approach that smacked of condescension was useless. A man must feel very dissatisfied with his past life and be prepared to sweep it all to one side if necessary. Religion could not be secondary to anything else. It could not, for instance, be tacked on to a life devoted to money-making. 'You cannot serve God and money,' Jesus declared. In serving God, a man may certainly make money but he must regard himself as its steward rather than its owner.

Secondly, a man must be prepared to take one step into the unknown by himself – the step of absolute faith. Arguments about religion actually prove nothing; faith proves everything. Jesus continually emphasised this. 'I tell you this,' he said, 'unless you turn round and become like children, you will never enter the Kingdom of Heaven.'

But once a man fulfilled these conditions, the Reign of God could begin in his life. The evidence of it would be that God's spirit would guide him; his prayers, which would be mainly to discover God's will, would be answered; his life would be filled with useful service and death would be the gateway to closer union with God.

A more sombre side of Jesus's teaching is his attitude to those who rejected him. They judge themselves, he said. They prefer the darkness to the light because their deeds are evil. Perhaps more than any other religious teacher, Jesus saw the terrible power of sin in men's lives. 'The gate is wide that leads to perdition,' he declared, 'there is plenty of room on the road, and many go that way.' In a world needing so desperately the services of the Good Samaritan, he bitterly condemned the selfish and useless life, and all those who added to the suffering and misery of mankind.

In the Sermon on the Mount and elsewhere Jesus gives many examples of how his followers would behave. They would have a deep respect for the sacredness of marriage and family life; they would give generously and secretly to those in need; they would respect their enemies and be prepared 'to turn the other cheek'. And for general guidance he gave the Golden Rule, 'Always treat others as you would like them to treat you.'

In place of the 613 rules laid down by the Scribes of his day, Jesus gave two: love God and love your neighbour. But according to Jesus the one is dependent on the other. To live the Christian life we need the Christian faith, for it is God within us who can best inspire love for our fellow-men.

# Christianity

## 16. The Christian Church

'The Kingdom of Heaven is like mustard seed which a man took and sowed in his field. As a seed, mustard is smaller than any other; but when it is grown it is bigger than any garden plant.' If these words of Jesus were a prophecy of the growth of Christianity, they certainly came true. From the eleven men he left in Jerusalem, Christianity has grown into by far the most widely accepted religion in the world, numbering about 1200,000,000 adherents.

### The early years

The fifth book of the New Testament, 'The Acts of the Apostles', describes the energy and determination with which the eleven disciples, or apostles, spread the Christian faith. From the Day of Pentecost when they felt the Holy Spirit, promised by Jesus, descend upon them, they worked unceasingly, and converts soon numbered many thousands. Among them appeared a brilliant young rabbi, Paul of Tarsus, who took Christianity into Europe and eventually reached Rome, where, it is said, he perished during the persecutions of Nero. In a letter he describes his sufferings during his missionary work: he was imprisoned many times, beaten eight times, shipwrecked three times, stoned, constantly exposed to cold and hunger and the fear of assassination. But he never faltered. Such was the spirit of the men who pioneered Christianity in the early years.

At first they were persecuted by their fellow-countrymen, the Jews; later, by the Romans. Through persecution they had been driven underground, and the Romans suspected them of being a secret society plotting against the state. It was therefore easy for Nero to blame them for the fire of Rome. Later, when everyone was required to acknowledge the Roman emperor as one of the gods, the Christians refused to do so and were promptly put to death by various ingenious means: they were burnt alive, sawn in two, or thrown to the lions. Faced with this horrible fate many Christians gave up their faith, but strangely enough their numbers continued to grow. Finally, when Rome abandoned the struggle against them and in 380 acknowledged Christianity as the only official religion of the Empire, one-sixth of its population had already been converted.

During these early years the People of the Way, as Christians were first called, were organized into what is now known as 'the Church' (from a Greek word meaning 'house of the Lord'). The Christian congregations throughout the Empire were grouped into districts over which a bishop presided. Eventually, the Bishop of Rome was acknowledged as 'first among equals'. He was later called 'Pope' or 'Father'.

It was also necessary at this time to define Christianity, as many people either received an imperfect account of it or tried to alter it according to their own whims. Church Councils were held and there emerged from them three statements of faith. The most important is known as 'the Apostles' Creed'. It is over 1,800 years old, but still remains the basis of Christian faith. Many Christians today, while accepting the historic details, will look upon some of the descriptive language as symbolic.

'I believe in God the Father Almighty, maker of heaven and earth:

And in Jesus Christ His only Son our Lord, who was conceived by the Holy Ghost, born of the Virgin Mary, suffered under Pontius Pilate, was crucified, dead and buried, he descended into hell; the third day he rose again from the dead, he ascended into heaven and sitteth on the right hand of God the Father Almighty; from thence he shall come to judge the quick and the dead.

I believe in the Holy Ghost, the Holy Catholic Church; the communion of saints; the forgiveness of sins; the resurrection of the body and the life everlasting.'

The Church continued to grow. In the fourth century it reached Abyssinia and Ireland, and in the fifth century Britain, in the sixth century Germany, in the eighth century the Netherlands, and in the ninth century the Slav countries and Scandinavia.

## The Middle Ages

The Middle Ages may conjure up visions of minstrels, knights in shining armour, mystery plays, fairs, and revels. But for the common people life was often grim and harsh. They suffered servitude, poverty, and the constant fear of plagues and other deadly diseases. The Church was now rich and powerful and had lost much of the kindly and gentle spirit of its founder.

It was oppressed by many problems, not least the rise of Islam, a new religion that spread along the shores of the Mediterranean and for a time overran the whole of Spain and southern France. Nine Christian crusades were fruitlessly undertaken to drive the Muslims out of Palestine. Even children took a hand in the campaign. In 1212 thousands of them set out for the Holy Land. None returned. They died either of disease or starvation, or were sold by Christian traders into slavery.

Many people found refuge from this brutish life in monasteries and convents. At first these religious orders worked and prayed hard under strict discipline and were greatly respected for their learning and their service to the community. Later, they became very rich. In England in Henry VIII's reign it was estimated that they owned a third of the country's wealth. But gradually discipline was relaxed and monks and nuns became noted for their laziness and ignorance.

Another bad feature of the Middle Ages was the Church's intolerance of those who would not accept its teaching. Everywhere Jews were persecuted and under Christian rulers suffered the most appalling degradation and cruelty. In many countries the dreaded Inquisition secretly imprisoned, tortured, and destroyed heretics – people who held views contrary to those of the Church.

The popes themselves became wealthy princes, sometimes quarrelling with other rulers and setting a bad example to their fellow Christians. Bishops neglected their duties; priests, their parishes. During the Black Death in England many priests simply abandoned their people and fled for safety to London.

Few people knew what the teaching of Jesus was about as they had little instruction and the gospels were not translated into their own language. Superstition took the place of faith in God. Men trudged miles to worship at the shrines of saints, to gaze on holy relics and wonder-working images. There were probably enough 'Pieces of the True Cross' in Europe to build a battleship.

Yet Christian charity had by no means disappeared. The monasteries provided free shelter for the poor traveller and medical treatment for the sick. The Church provided sanctuary for the fugitive from violence. Once he was within its walls his enemies could not touch him, and the Church would hear his case and dispense justice. There were, of course, many conscientious priests and, in all ranks, saintly people who tried to relieve the harshness and ignorance of the times. Notable among them were humble men like Francis of Assisi, who founded an order of travelling preachers or friars sworn to poverty, chastity, and obedience. These friars tramped through Europe preaching the Christian message of love and peace to eager crowds. But generally the Church was failing badly to reflect either the teaching or the spirit of Jesus Christ, and reform was bound to come.

## The divisions in the Church

In 1053 there took place a serious division in the Church. When the Emperor Constantine built the city of Constantinople (now Istanbul) in the fourth century, it took the place of Rome as the governing centre of the Empire. Over the centuries the Bishops of Constantinople became increasingly important and they began to quarrel with the Pope in Rome, who assumed that he should have the final word on every matter. There were many differences of opinion and finally the whole of the eastern part of the Church refused allegiance to the Pope and became independent. It has remained so ever since and is known as the Orthodox Church. It consists of a federation of independent groups of churches, each presided over by a Patriarch. The Patriarch of Constantinople is recognized as senior, but the Russian Church was and still remains the largest single unit within the Orthodox Church. The western half of the Church is called 'the Catholic Church', or more accurately 'the Roman Catholic Church', since the word 'Catholic' means universal and it is so used in the Apostles' Creed.

The Reformation came four hundred years later, in the fifteenth century. Martin Luther is the chief name associated with it. It was his bold plea for reform which triggered off a general protest against the unchristian teaching and practices of the Church. Once people were able to read the gospels for themselves, they realised how far the Church had failed. Only when it became evident that its rulers were opposed to reform did new churches begin to appear. Some were based on the interpretation of Christianity by Luther, others on the work of another reformer, Calvin. These churches became known as 'the Protestant Churches', from the word 'to protest'. They taught that the Bible alone was necessary for the understanding of Christianity, and that a man's salvation depended solely on his own personal faith in Christ. Britain became Protestant in the reign of Henry VIII when he broke with Rome over his divorce. The Church of England never accepted the Pope again and the British monarch still remains the head of the English Church.

After the Reformation the Roman Catholic Church began an internal reform. The popes ceased to be politicians and a great religious revival took place, though the Inquisition still remained.

Unfortunately the spirit of intolerance that we saw rising in the Middle Ages continued, and great bitterness arose between Protestants and Roman Catholics. Whichever church gained the upper hand persecuted the other one, and thousands of people perished for their faith. In England, when the Church of England was established, the laws against those who would not conform to its teaching were very harsh. Many people found it impossible to live in this country and, like the Pilgrim Fathers in 1620, left it to begin a new life elsewhere.

## The present situation

Slowly, very slowly, Christians began to learn to live together again in peace. In Britain many different churches were allowed to exist apart from the Church of England. They are known today as the Free Churches, that is, free from state control. They have grown in size and many of them have spread to other countries, especially America.

One of the oldest is the Congregational Church. It began four hundred years ago when Congregationalists were first known as Independents. They did not believe that a church should be governed by a king or by bishops. Each congregation should have an independent life without interference from outside. The earliest Congregationalists were terribly persecuted and it was from their numbers that the Pilgrim Fathers came.

The Baptist Church began in 1612. Baptists were Independents who believed that infant baptism was contrary to the Bible. In the Baptist Church only adults are baptized, and the ceremony takes place in front of the whole church as a sign of personal commitment to the Christian life.

The Presbyterian Church is based on the teaching of Calvin. The highest officials are called presbyters, not bishops. It is the national Church of Scotland, but there are many Presbyterian churches in other countries.

The Methodist Church was founded in the eighteenth century by John Wesley, a Church of England clergyman. Wesley protested because his church was not reaching the masses of the people. During his preaching campaigns he travelled a quarter of a million miles on horseback through England, and thousands of people were converted.

The Salvation Army was a breakaway from the Methodist Church. It was founded by William Booth in 1865 and has always aimed to give practical help to the very poor. It is organized on military lines; its officers are subject to orders and adopt military ranks, such as captain, major, and general.

There are many interesting smaller churches, such as the Society of Friends (Quakers), who are pacifists and great social workers, the Plymouth Brethren and the Pentecostalists. Anyone in the United Kingdom is free to found a church, build a mission hall, and worship in any way he pleases.

Church buildings themselves vary in size and beauty from vast cathedrals and abbeys to the smallest of bare 'preaching houses'.

Worship is congregational and generally open to the public. Worshippers meet at certain hours, mainly on Sundays, sing hymns and pray together, listen to scripture readings and a talk (sermon) usually given by the priest or minister. An important additional service held regularly and known variously as The Mass, the Eucharist, Holy Communion or the Lord's Supper commemorates the death of Jesus. Bread and wine are shared together as at Jesus's last supper with his disciples. Children attend Sunday Schools where worship and teaching are suited to the various age groups. Week evenings are used for study groups, youth clubs and other social, charitable and religious activities, including training classes for church membership.

Both men and women are to be found within the monastic orders of the Church. Some orders are closed and have little contact with the outside world; others serve humanity in different ways, providing teachers, missionaries and medical services in many parts of the world.

The three great festivals of the Christian Church are Easter, commemorating the death and resurrection of Jesus, Christmas, his birth, and Whitsun, the special gift of the Holy Spirit. These are joyful occasions and many Churches are beautifully decorated to celebrate them.

In the eighteenth and nineteenth centuries there was a tremendous upsurge of missionary activity. Missionary societies were formed and the Bible translated into hundreds of different languages (1,280 at the time of writing). William Carey went to India, Robert Morrison to China, David Livingstone to Africa, John Williams to the South Seas, and Wilfred Grenfell to Labrador. These were part of the vanguard of thousands of Christian missionaries who spread all over the world. They were followed by doctors, nurses, and teachers in such numbers that over great areas not a single school or hospital existed which was not built and staffed by the Christian Church.

Meanwhile at home, Christians played an important part in social reform. They actively engaged in the early struggle for better housing and industrial conditions for the working classes. 'British Socialism,' declared Morgan Philips, 'owed far more to Methodism than to Marxism.' In this century the churches have fought tyranny. Professor Einstein stated that when Hitler rose to power in Germany, first the universities and then the press gave in to him. 'Only the Church', he continued, 'stood squarely across the path of Hitler's campaign for suppressing truth. I never had any special interest in the Church before, but now I feel a great affection and admiration: the Church alone has had the courage and persistence to stand for intellectual truth and moral freedom.'

In recent years, however, the Church in the west has

declined. The terrible loss of life in both world wars and the general upheaval that followed it slowly reduced church membership. In addition the rise of Communism behind the Iron Curtain and elsewhere has taken its toll. No less than thirty governments are anti-religious and require atheism to be taught to all children in school. More than half the population of the world lives in countries where religious activity is severely restricted. But persecution has not destroyed the Church. In Russia, for example, after nearly seventy years of atheist education the Orthodox Church claims a membership of fifty million, three times the size of the communist party.

A further serious cause of decline has been the growth in non-communist countries of materialism (devotion to worldly prosperity) and secularism (questioning of religious beliefs). This has resulted in widespread indifference to religion. Nevertheless, the Church continues its mission of teaching, contributing large funds and devoted workers to charity at home, Christian missions abroad, and practical aid to the Third World.

While Christianity in the west declines, it advances elsewhere, notably in Africa and South America. In many countries, too, which were once part of colonial empires, the Churches are now independent and very active in 'spreading the Gospel'. They themselves have about thirty thousand missionaries at work at home and abroad. There is, in fact, an organised Christian Church in every inhabited country in the world, and more than twenty million people are converted every year to the Christian faith.

Perhaps the greatest weakness of the Christian Church through its history has been intolerance, both within its ranks and towards non-Christians. This spirit seems gradually to be disappearing. There is now a World Council of Churches and a closer relationship between Roman Catholics and Protestants. With this desire for unity also comes the urge among Christians to express their faith and worship in terms better suited to the twentieth century.

# From the Christian Scriptures

God loved the world so much that he gave his only Son, that everyone who has faith in him may not die but have eternal life.

(John 3:16)

If anyone wishes to be a follower of mine, he must leave self behind; he must take up his cross and come with me. Whoever cares for his own safety is lost; but if a man will let himself be lost for my sake, he will find his true self. What will a man gain by winning the whole world at the cost of his true self?

(Matthew 16:24)

Ask, and you will receive; seek, and you will find; knock, and the door will be opened.

(Sermon on the Mount)

You have learned that they were told, 'Love your neighbour, hate your enemy.' But what I tell you is this: Love your enemies and pray for your persecutors; only so can you be children of your heavenly Father, who makes his sun rise on good and bad alike, and sends the rain on the honest and the dishonest.

(Sermon on the Mount)

Jesus said, 'It is easier for a camel to pass through the eye of a needle than for a rich man to enter the kingdom of God.' The disciples were amazed to hear this. 'Then who can be saved?' they asked. Jesus looked them in the face, and said:

'For men this is impossible; but everything is possible for God.'

(Matthew 19:24)

For I am convinced that there is nothing in death or life, in the realm of spirits or superhuman powers, in the world as it is or the world as it shall be, in the forces of the universe, in heights or depths – nothing in all creation that can separate us from the love of God in Christ Jesus our Lord.

(Romans 8:38)

Set your troubled hearts at rest. Trust in God always: trust also in me. There are many dwelling-places in my Father's house; if it were not so I should have told you; for I am going there on purpose to prepare a place for you. And if I go and prepare a place for you, I shall come again and receive you to myself, so that where I am you may be also.

(John 14:1)

# Points for discussion

1 What kind of Messiah would have been most popular with the Jews? Why do you think Jesus chose quite a different role?

2 Were the charges brought against Jesus before Caiaphas and Pilate true? Could you justify in any way the actions of these two men over the trial of Jesus?

3 What did Jesus teach about suffering? Why does suffering sometimes lead to a stronger faith in God?

4 What was it, do you think, that convinced the disciples that Jesus was in some special way God in human form? Do you think any other conclusion possible?

5 Tertullian, one of the early Christian leaders, declared, 'The more you mow us down the more we grow.' Why did the persecution of the Christian Church have exactly the opposite effect to what was intended?

6 What value has the Christian church in the world today? How can it improve on this?

# Islam

## 17. The life of Muhammad

Arabia is the largest peninsula in the world and it is mostly desert. There are prosperous towns in the coastal areas and a fertile district in the south-west, known as the Yemen. But apart from these features and a high plateau where the famous Arab horses are bred there are only vast sandy wastes and occasional oases. Consequently, Arabia has not been very important in world affairs except for one outstanding event: Muhammad, the founder of the last of the world's great religions, was born there.

This religion is called Islam and its followers are known as Muslims or Moslems. The word 'Islam' is also used to denote the Muslim brotherhood throughout the world, which now numbers nine hundred million. There are few Muslims in Europe except in the south-east corner, but great numbers live in North Africa, Egypt, and the Middle East. Far beyond this in Asiatic Russia, Pakistan, India, China, Malaya, and Indonesia they number many millions. Though scattered over the world, they are united in three articles of faith: they believe that there is only one god, that Muhammad was his greatest prophet, and that he gave to them the sacred scriptures known as the Qur'an.

### Muhammad's early life

Muhammad was born about 570 in the most celebrated city of Arabia, Mecca. For a thousand years or more before Muhammad it had been a sacred city frequented by pilgrims. Within it was the ancient temple known as the *Ka'bah*, containing altars to many gods, and there also was the famous Black Stone which was said to have fallen from heaven.

Except for its pagan altars it remains exactly the same today, forbidden territory to all but Muslims.

Muhammad was an orphan reared by his uncle. He became a camel-driver and at the age of twenty-five married his employer, Khadijah, a wealthy widow fifteen years his senior. He was very fond of her and married no one else while she was alive. After his marriage he continued to travel across Arabia, meeting many strangers, among whom were both Jews and Christians. He eagerly inquired about their religion.

At the age of forty he became unsettled and troubled in mind. He gave up camel-driving and wandered about the countryside near his home. One day, as he rested in a cave, he had a frightening experience. First he saw the eyes, then gradually the outline of a strange, unearthly being whom he later recognized as the Angel Gabriel. In letters of fire he received a command to declare the message that the angel would give him. At first he was terrified, but these visions were constantly repeated and at last Muhammad realized that he was called to be a prophet of God. And so for many years afterwards, from time to time, he received in this way the word of God. His friends wrote it down as he repeated it and it is preserved today as the Qur'an.

It was unfortunate for Muhammad that he happened to be born into the Quraish tribe. This tribe was in charge of the holy places in Mecca and made a regular income from the pilgrims who visited the *Ka'bah*. Now Muhammad's message was that the worship of any deity bar Allah (the Muslim name for God) was a sin and that the pagan altars which the pilgrims visited should be destroyed. The result was inevitable. He was hated by his own people, and when his uncle died he was outlawed by them. At the same time his wife died, and he was left friendless and in constant danger of assassination.

It happened, however, that a certain town, Medina (then known as Yathrib), which lay 250 miles to the north of

Mecca, was in turmoil. The clans were constantly quarrelling, and they needed a stranger to act as a judge and settle their differences for them. Some pilgrims from Medina were greatly impressed by Muhammad and his message, and invited him to go to Medina and restore order. Muhammad gladly accepted the invitation. He knew, however, that he could not make the journey safely in daylight. Members of his own tribe would kill him. So he escaped from Mecca by night, hid in a cave for four days, and finally completed his flight (hijra) to Medina by a little-known route. He was so popular when he arrived that every clan offered him a home. Rather than offend anyone he said, 'I will build my house where my camel stops.' The house which he eventually built is preserved today as a mosque in memory of him. The year of his arrival, C.E. 622, dates as Year 1 (A.H.) in the Muslim calendar.

## The conquest of Mecca

As soon as Muhammad was firmly settled in Medina he turned his thoughts again to his home town, Mecca. It was the ancient centre of religion for the whole of Arabia, and Muhammad knew that neither his teaching nor his influence could spread successfully through the country unless Mecca accepted him. To win Mecca would need careful planning. It would be no use, for instance, to defeat the Meccans in a great battle and take possession of the city. He could not conquer and be hated; he must conquer and be welcome.

He began his campaign by attacking the caravans travelling north from Mecca. These attacks were small, involving perhaps a dozen men, but they served to irritate the Meccans and remind them that Muhammad was very much alive. Gradually this interference with Meccan trade became more frequent and resulted sometimes in pitched battles, which Muhammad won. On one occasion he was in mortal danger, and was lucky to escape with a few gashes and the loss of two teeth.

Eventually the Meccans became exasperated and decided to get rid of Muhammad once and for all. They sent a force of ten thousand against Medina. But Muhammad, employing an expert spy system, had good notice of their coming. He halted them outside Medina with a deep, wide trench that defied the most skilful horsemanship, and before they had devised a means of overcoming this obstacle, the rains came and forced them home without even having engaged the enemy. When the news got about, everybody laughed at their humiliation and the Meccans lost much of their influence and trade.

A year later Muhammad set out on a pilgrimage to Mecca. When the Meccans heard of it they sent two hundred horsemen to bar his way. Muhammad did not fight; he merely sat down and argued with them. In the end they made a treaty which allowed him to visit the city. He had, by then, many converts in Mecca, and when he made his pilgrimage, he showed such reverence towards the *Ka'bah* and the Black Stone that he won nearly everyone's approval. So shortly afterwards when he arrived again with an army, after a slight show of opposition they opened the gates and let him in. The conquest of Mecca was complete.

*Muhammad and the Jews*

Two centuries before Muhammad, Roman persecutions accounted for many thousands of Jews seeking refuge in Arabia. They were clever and more industrious than the Arabs themselves, and soon owned the best of the land and property. Half the population of Medina was Jewish.

Muhammad planned to unite the Jews and Arabs through his new religion. He accepted the Jewish Bible, its long succession of prophets, and Jesus of Nazareth also. All he wished was to be known as the last and greatest of God's messengers. He ordered his followers to face the holy city of Jerusalem when they prayed and to observe the Jewish fast of the Atonement. In this way he hoped to win the Jews. Many rulers in the past had tried to alter the Jewish faith but they had all failed. So did Muhammad. The Jews declared that much in the Qur'an was false and that Muhammad was not a prophet at all.

This attitude infuriated Muhammad. Turning against the Jews he determined to get rid of them by expulsion, slavery, or murder. They suffered very severely and on one occasion a Jewess who had lost all her menfolk tried to poison him. Fortunately, he took only one mouthful of the roasted lamb she offered him. This incident did not improve relationships, which, since that day, have grown worse through political as well as religious differences. The problem as to who has the legal right to occupy Palestine seems insoluble.

After the conquest of Mecca and with the gradual disappearance of the Jews, Muhammad was in a masterful position. He swept rapidly through the country uniting the people under Moslem rule. Then quite suddenly, in 10 A.H., he died. But he had worked with such zeal and intelligence that he had laid the foundation of a religion that was to challenge most of the known world and to subdue nearly half the continent of Europe.

## Muhammad as a man

As a man, Muhammad was striking in appearance. He was powerfully built, broad across the shoulders, long in the arms, with rough hands and feet. His eyes were sharp and intelligent, his nose hooked, his hair thick, and his beard long and luxuriant. He moved clumsily, like a man walking downhill. He spoke little and never without a purpose.

His early visions changed his character. From being a quiet and little-known camel-driver he suddenly developed into a prophet with a burning message of salvation. He declared in fact that those who refused to accept his teaching would most certainly go to hell. As he became more powerful his message began to change into one which showed shrewd thinking rather than emotional fervour. The Qur'an itself reflects this change in outlook.

He had qualities which are not usual in a great religious leader. A fearless fighter, he did not hesitate to encourage the use of the sword against opposition and unbelief. We see this in his treatment of the Jews, which did not seem to reflect his own teaching about the compassion and mercy of God. He had many wives. At one time they became so troublesome to him that he left home for a while. He also acquired much wealth, but never showed it in his way of life.

But these things were not important to him. He did not teach the value of poverty or chastity, nor did he consider himself a perfect example of the good life. He frequently spoke about his own need for the forgiveness and mercy of God. His chief aim was to overthrow paganism and to unite his people in the worship of one God, and this he did with universal success.

# Islam

## 18. The faith and customs of Islam

The Qur'an was slowly completed over twenty-three years of
Muhammad's life. It consisted entirely of the revelations he
received during this period. Many of them, he confessed, were
preceded by a painful physical experience, a slow, dull throb-
bing in the head as of a muffled bell. Consequently, he grew to
hate the sound of bells in ordinary life and they were never
used in Islam, either to summon men to worship or to assist
them in their devotions.

Muhammad always spoke of the Qur'an with reverence. It
was not his work, he believed, but the word of God, dictated to
the world through him. Once when his critics challenged him
to work a miracle in order to prove the truth of his teaching, he
retorted that this was quite unnecessary. The Qur'an itself
was the supreme miracle. If they doubted it, let them try to
compose ten verses that could compare with it! And ever
since his death, his followers have accepted it as the sacred
revelation of God's will. During its reading no Muslim will
speak, smoke, eat, or drink, and young children are taught to
repeat it so that by the age of ten many of them can recite most
of its 114 chapters. Though the English translation makes
dull reading, the sound of the Qur'an recited in Arabic is very
beautiful indeed.

As we have seen, the teaching of Muhammad was so closely
connected with the Jewish and Christian faiths that it could
hardly be called a new religion. Muhammad traced the origin
of the Arab race to Abraham through his son Ishmael. He
accepted the teaching of the great Hebrew prophets and, for
the most part, the teaching of Jesus. He refused to believe,
however, that Jesus was crucified and declared that the
crucifixion story was a lie invented by the Jews, but the

134

Christians he denounced as idolaters because they worshipped Jesus as God. There should be only one religion, and Jews and Christians should renounce the teaching in the Bible that Muhammad disliked. This, however, proved quite impossible. No Jew, for example, could believe that his forefathers worshipped God and Ezra; neither could a Christian accept that Jesus was born under a palm tree and declared from his cradle, 'I am the servant of God', nor that the Holy Trinity consisted of God, Jesus, and the Virgin Mary.

Islam spread with remarkable rapidity despite Muhammad's failure to win the support of the Jews and Christians in Arabia. Its basic teaching, found in the Qur'an and in the traditions that developed after Muhammad's death, is about the nature of God.

## Allah, the all-powerful

Five times each day throughout the world of Islam, Muslims are called to prayer with these words, 'Allah is most great; I bear witness that there is no god but Allah. . . .' In its original form, *Al-Ilah*, meant the One God, the Strong, the Mighty One, and it is strength and power that one always associates with Allah. He made all things, and man is his servant. His absolute power demands absolute obedience, and to defy him is to be in danger of everlasting punishment. The Qur'an sternly condemns all who refuse to accept the will of Allah, and justifies 'the Holy War' against unbelievers, who often were given the choice of accepting the Muslim religion or death.

Allah, however, has other qualities than power. He is merciful and kind to those in need. Muhammad had often observed in his native town of Mecca that the rich neglected the poor and that widows and orphans (of whom he was one) were left destitute. The Qur'an condemns such callousness. Muslims are expected by Allah to give generously to those in need and not to flaunt their wealth in the face of poverty.

Allah, though the creator of the universe, watches over every detail of daily life. 'He is nearer to a man than the veins of his neck', and whatever good luck or misfortune befalls him is to be regarded as a sign of Allah's favour or displeasure.

In his efforts to save mankind Allah is assisted by many angels. Three thousand work with him, and in addition every man has his own guardian angel. There are also lesser creatures called djinns, some who assist man in living the good life and others whose influence on man is wholly evil.

Finally, Allah will one day judge mankind. Every man who ever lived must appear before him and an account of his life will be given by his guardian angel. His deeds will be weighed in the balance before his eyes and on the result he will be committed to heaven or hell.

The vivid descriptions that are found in the Qur'an of angels and the Judgement, heaven and hell have been accepted literally by generations of Muslims. Today, we are inclined to think of them as symbolic pictures of the power, mercy, and justice of Allah.

## The Five Pillars of the Faith

Every Muslim has for his guidance what are known as the Five Pillars of the Faith. These are five primary duties that he must always keep in mind and try to carry out.

First there is the recital of the Muslim creed (Al Shahada): 'There is no God but Allah and Muhammad is his prophet.' The special importance of Muhammad must be acknowledged. Abraham was the first Muslim, Moses gave the Law, David the Psalms, Jesus the Gospel, but Muhammad gave the final revelation.

The second pillar is worship (Al Salat). The Qur'an requires an act of worship three times a day, but common practice has made it five. A Muslim must wash each time before he prays, but in the desert he is allowed to use sand. Then facing Mecca he must prostrate himself before Allah. This prostration is accompanied by a series of dramatic gestures, beginning with the hands, open, the thumbs touching the lobes of the ears, and ending with the worshipper forward on his knees with his face to the ground. In the course of a day a Muslim will perform this action seventeen times, during which he recites words of adoration to Allah.

A third pillar of the faith is fasting (Al Saoum). During the ninth lunar month of each year the celebrated Fast of Ramadan is held. Throughout this month a Muslim must not smoke, eat, drink, or have sexual intercourse between sunrise and sunset each day. We can readily understand how difficult it is to keep this rule in very hot climates.

The giving of alms (Al Zakat) is another pillar of the faith. This must be done by all Muslims who are normally able to afford it. Some governments have, in fact, levied a tax of two and a half pence in the pound, which could not easily be avoided. But, in any case, in Islam the giving of charity is done quite openly as an acknowledgement that all wealth comes from God. If a man has done wrong, he is more likely to be forgiven if he gives extra money to the poor or even to his relatives.

The final pillar of the faith is pilgrimage (Al Haj). Every good Muslim should aim to go to Mecca and to the tomb of the prophet in Medina at least once in his lifetime. Special conditions apply to this pilgrimage. The head must be shaved, special clothes worn, and nails and hair must not be cut from the outset of the pilgrimage until the return journey is begun. In Mecca, once the pilgrim has arrived, there is an elaborate ritual to follow, including kissing the famous Black Stone and going round the *Ka'bah* seven times.

## Various customs and regulations

As in Judaism, there are regulations about food. All meat must be slaughtered and prepared in a special way, and certain foods, including pork, are prohibited.

Other prohibitions include drinking, gambling, usury, idolatry and extra-marital sex. With regard to usury, it is interesting to note that no less than three of the world's great religions condemned it, yet modern Western economy is based upon it.

It is clear from the Qur'an that the most important member

of the community is the free, male Muslim. Islam has been for many centuries a slave society. Muhammad himself kept slaves and laid down rules for their treatment. The sphere of women, as in other religions, is the house, the bearing and nurture of children and the welfare of the family. According to the Qur'an, a man may have up to four wives provided he can look after them adequately. He should treat all his wives equally and if he cannot, should only marry one. He can also own concubines. During this century, however, many great changes have taken place, and Muslim women are acquiring much greater freedom than they enjoyed in days gone by.

The centre of Muslim worship is the mosque. Mosques are often beautiful buildings with fountains, cloisters, and rich mosaic work. Many of them have one or more minarets, slender towers from the top of which the muezzin, or mosque crier, calls the population to prayer. Inside the mosque there is always a niche (mihrab) which indicates the direction of Mecca. The prayer leader, known as the Imam, together with the congregation, faces Mecca, and in complete unison they prostrate themselves and repeat the words of adoration from the Qur'an. Normally, a Muslim says his prayers wherever he happens to be when he hears the summons from the minaret, but on Fridays at noon he is expected to be in the mosque if it is at all possible.

There are a number of festivals and special occasions during the year. New Year falls approximately in October. It celebrates the journey of Muhammad to Medina (Hijra) and the beginning of his ministry there. Two months later the birth and life of Muhammad occupies a four week celebration. Two important occasions are linked with Ramadan in or near the month of June. The Night of Power (Lailat al Qadr) towards the end of the Fast celebrates the giving of the Qur'an, and at the close of Ramadan there is great rejoicing when gifts are made to the poor and presents are given in the family and to relatives and friends. Finally, the end of the month of pilgrimage (September) is also celebrated throughout Islam.

# Islam

## 19. The rise and fall of the Muslim Empire

Muhammad's death in June 632 C.E. was a sudden and terrible blow to his followers. It is a remarkable tribute to him that after only ten years in Medina he inspired a great religious movement that was to dominate most of the known world. His place was taken by deputies, or caliphs, who were at first as devoted to Islam as the prophet himself. Under brilliant generalship the armies of Arabia, within eight years, swept through Syria, Persia, Palestine, and Egypt. The Muslim Empire was born.

### The Empire

There were at least two good reasons for the rapid growth of the Empire. The great powers which alternately controlled Arabia were Persia and Byzantium (the eastern half of the old Roman Empire). Both were at this time weak and the people they governed uneasy and dissatisfied. So when the Arabs appeared they were often greeted with hopeful curiosity rather than hostility.

A second reason for success was the sensible and kindly way in which the early Muslims treated the foreigner. The picture of cruelty and violence that is associated with Islam belongs to a later age. The invaders were in fact much kinder to those they conquered than Muhammad himself had been to the Arabian Jews. A Christian writer of the period states that they praised Christianity, honoured its priests, and granted money and privileges to its churches and monasteries. They proudly declared that John the Baptist was buried beneath their mosque in Damascus. They referred to Christ as 'Our Lord Jesus' and his mother as 'Our Lady Mary'.

THE REMARKABLE GROWTH OF ISLAM *the first hundred years*

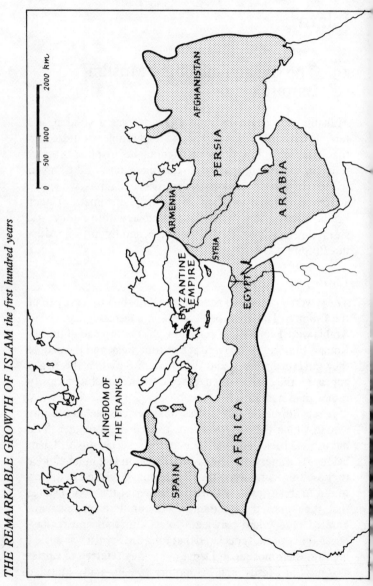

So the teaching of Muhammad spread: to the west through Spain into France and to the east as far as India. Under its strong and peaceful rule, commerce, industry, and science flourished. Spain, for example, enjoyed prosperity for centuries, thousands were converted to the Muslim faith, and even the Jews, so often ill-treated, lived peaceful and happy lives there.

The Muslim Empire, however, like its predecessor, the Roman Empire, was destined to fall and for similar reasons. It grew careless of the dangers that surrounded it and fell a victim to the barbarian. Baghdad had become the centre of Islam. The caliphs were renowned for their 'Arabian Nights' splendour and, cosseted by luxury, they quite forgot their duties as the representatives of the stern and vigilant prophet Muhammad. So when hordes of Asiatic tribesmen invaded Persia the caliph was immediately defeated and the whole country overrun. It says much for the civilizing power of Islam that when the fighting was over, the invaders were so impressed by the power of Muslim law that they accepted it and later were themselves converted to the faith.

But this was only the first of many terrible invasions that the Empire suffered. In the thirteenth century the Mongol brigand Jenghis Ghan sacked Persia and the country also suffered two disastrous epidemics of the Black Death. About the same time Turkish tribesmen from Asia invaded the Balkans and occupied the land now known as Turkey. Though they too became Muslims, they retained much of the brutality of their former life. In 1394, for example, after defeating a Christian army at Nicopolis, they butchered ten thousand prisoners in one day for the pleasure of the Sultan. It was this kind of ruthless barbarism that gave Islam so bad a reputation.

The Turks prospered while the rest of the Arab world declined. Muslim power in Spain had virtually disappeared by the end of the fifteenth century, though the great Mogul Empire in India lasted another three hundred years. Turkey became the centre of Muslim power when Persia declined, and continued to wield an influence until the end of the First World War. But though Islam gradually ceased to be a great political power, the millions converted to its religion have nearly all remained faithful to it ever since.

## Sects and heresies

Every religion tends to drift away from its founder and form separate groups differing in belief and customs. In Islam many sects arose, some harmless, others intolerant, and we shall consider briefly those which have left a permanent mark upon the Muslim world.

Trouble began with the caliphs in Baghdad. They became worldly minded and indifferent to the religion they were supposed to control. Consequently, a sect known as the Kharijites appeared, who declared that the true test of a genuine caliph was his character. It did not matter what country, tribe, or clan he came from as long as he lived a morally perfect life. They remained the puritans of Islam, and today we find their imprint on the Muslim religion in southern Algeria, Oman, Zanzibar, and Arabia.

A more powerful sect were the Shi'ites. Their view was the exact opposite of the Kharijites'. The caliph's morals mattered very little; the all-important qualification was that he should be a descendant of the Prophet. As a consequence there was much quarrelling and bloodshed about the Succession.

Years later some Shi'ites were declaring that there had been only twelve true caliphs or imams (leaders) as they preferred to call them, and that the last one, El-Mahdi, would return one day as Messiah to the Muslim world. This form of Shi'ism has been the official religion of Iran since 1499. Other Shi'ites, known as Ismaelis, believed in only seven imams.

From the Ismaelis sprang an interesting religious order known as the Assassins. This word comes from *hashishin*, meaning hemp-eaters. Hemp or hashish has an intoxicating effect, and the weird dreams and visions it induces can render the victims completely obedient to their masters. The Assassins undertook murder as a religious duty and were drugged in this way before they were given their assignments. Their leader was known as 'the Old Man of the Mountains'. In Syria and the Lebanon they terrorised the Crusaders. Fortunately, the order was virtually wiped out in the thirteenth century. Some members, however, survived, because rulers in those days found the services of a professional assassin quite helpful in an emergency. A small peaceful community still survives in India. The Aga Khan, whom millions of Muslims accept as their spiritual leader, traces his descent to the last of the grand masters of the Assassins.

Arabia, the home of Islam, is today dominated by a sect known as Wahhabis. They are very strict, banning the wearing of costly clothes and ornaments, and prohibiting smoking, gambling, and music. A modern sect founded in the nineteenth century is the Bahai, whose main aim is to unite all religions and establish world brotherhood. Small missionary groups of Bahais are found in America and Europe.

Despite these differences of belief, the Muslim brotherhood remains a reality. The vast majority of Muslims are known as Sunnis, those that follow the ancient customs. They are normally peaceful and tolerant, and will not resort to warfare unless attacked. They are divided into four 'schools' which differ in their practices. To one of these every Muslim must belong, but they all recognise one another.

The most important movement in Islam, however, was Sufism. The teaching about Allah in the Qur'an appears to have had one main defect. It left the worshipper too far away from his god. Private prayer was not encouraged, and although Allah looked after those who obeyed him, he remained distant and inscrutable. The words Islam and Muslim both derive from an Arabic word meaning 'to submit' or 'surrender'. In short, man was the slave of Allah rather than his friend.

143

So very early in the history of Islam new teachers appeared declaring that Allah had spoken personally to them and that he sought the friendship of man. These teachers became very popular and were known as Sufis, from the garment of wool (*suf*) which each wore. Like the holy men of Hinduism they practised meditation, and like the ancient Hebrew prophets they denounced the sins of the rich, the worldly minded caliphs, and the professional religious teachers, the ulama. The Sufis, who were regarded as heretics, were often seized by the authorities and put to death. They then became saints in the eyes of the common people, and their tombs centres for religious pilgrimages. Many books appeared describing their lives and devotions and are still widely read. Unfortunately movements like this tend to get out of hand, and Sufism acquired many superstitions. From it sprang the fakirs of India, the dancing dervishes, and, more frivolously, fire-walkers, glass-eaters, and snake-charmers.

Sufism aroused bitter opposition, and fighting broke out within Islam. Eventually a brilliant reformer, Ghazali, drew together the best elements in Sufism and the old religion. As a result, the worship of saints is widely practised today, wandering teachers (marabouts) are greatly revered, and the life of meditation plays a much bigger part in the religion of Islam. Prayer beads are used and there are ninety-nine beautiful names for Allah to be repeated.

## Modern Islam

For most of the Muslim world, however, the centuries up to the present one have brought little change. Five times a day mosque and minaret resounded to the muezzin's call, seraglio and harem maintained their magic and mystery, and the Muslim lived and died in peace and security. By western standards it was a backward existence, but the Muslim, though he had little, was content, and in old age and poverty he was cared for.

The twentieth century has brought great changes. Muslim

countries came into much closer contact with the West. The upheaval of two world wars and, later, the huge increase in wealth from oil revenues awakened a keen desire for change. Did modern western society offer a better way of life? Many Muslims thought so and found the ancient laws and customs of their religion a barrier to progress. Muslim law, for example, had been responsible for large areas of arable land lying waste. And how could a complicated prayer routine or the harem and the veil fit into the life of a modern city?

As a consequence, in Turkey, after the First World War the Sultan was deposed, the Caliphate abolished and under the dictatorship of Kemal Ataturk the State in 1928 became secular. Similar experiments followed elsewhere; in Egypt, and in Iran, for example, where the Shah, with the help of large foreign loans, set about modernising his country.

More recently, however, there has been a sharp reaction to these changes. The materialism of the West with its sexual freedoms, breakdowns of family life and increasing lawlessness, is far from the Muslim ideal, as also is atheistic Communism, and the ancient traditions of Islam are being revived.

In Muslim countries, Allah is recognized as the head of the state, the law is founded on the Qur'an and the family is regarded as essential to social order. All matters related to it, marriage, divorce, guardianship, inheritance, are decided by theologians and the resulting laws are administered by Islamic judges. In matters of public order it is felt that many of the problems that affect the western world can largely disappear if penalties for wrong doing are more severe and alcohol is prohibited.

Accordingly, in Egypt in 1971, an amendment to the Constitution made Islamic law the main source of legislation; in Pakistan the legal code and public practice are now in accordance with the old traditions; Turkey remains a secular state but the teaching of the Faith is compulsory in schools and the Islamic way of life is more generally accepted.

145

In Iran the Shah was deposed and strict Islamic rule restored, but the results there have been unfortunate. The Muslims in Iran are Shi'ites (see p 142) and very intolerant. Members of the Bahai faith have suffered great cruelty at their hands. They have also been at variance with the rest of Islam and have caused trouble especially during the annual pilgrimages to Mecca.

In India, however, the reverse has been true. Non-Hindus claim that they are treated as second class citizens. The sixty million Muslims there have frequently suffered from communal riots but, encouraged by the revival of Islam elsewhere, they have striven for equality and to preserve Urdu, their traditonal language. In China, Islam has re-awakened under a more tolerant government. In 1979 one hundred and fifty-eight mosques were re-opened.

It seems too that amongst the young there are those who welcome this return to tradition. In some cities, girl students have revived the use of the veil and young men have grown beards and refused to attend mixed parties. Mosque attendances have increased and hundreds of new mosques have been built. As a missionary religion Islam presents a serious rival in Africa to Christianity.

The power of Islam has certainly increased in recent years but can this return to fundamentalism, as it is called, be maintained? Not all Muslims are happy about it. In a changing world there is bound to be compromise. Muslim immigrants must conform, of course, to the laws of their adopted country. Where Muslims are in a minority, as in Kenya, Ghana and Tanzania, there is a similar situation: Muslim practice must adapt to the requirements of the State.

Nevertheless, in Muslim countries the tendency at present is towards a strict return to the ancient faith. Not a word of the Qur'an, we are told, has been changed in 1,400 years and the traditional way of life, based upon this timeless revelation, is being revived.

# From the Muslim Scriptures

Recite! in the name of thy Lord who created;
Created man from Clots of Blood;
Recite! For thy Lord is most beneficient,
Who hath taught the use of the pen,
Hath taught man that which he knew not.

          (The Angel Gabriel's call to Muhammad)

In the Name of God, the Merciful, the Compassionate.
Praise be to God, the Lord of the worlds,
The Merciful, and Compassionate.
King of the Day of Judgement.
Thee do we serve and on thee do we call for help,
Guide us on the straight path,
The paths of those to whom thou hast been gracious,
Not of those upon whom anger falls, or those who go
astray.

          (Prayer recited many times daily)

There is no piety in turning your faces towards the east or
the west, but he is pious who believeth in God and the last day
and the angels and the scriptures and the prophets; who for
the love of God disburseth his wealth to his kindred, and to
the orphans, and the needy, and the wayfarer, and those who
ask, and for ransoming; who observeth prayer, and payeth
the legal alms, and who is one of those who are faithful to
their engagements and patient under ills and hardships and in
time of trouble; these are they who are just, and these are they
who fear God.

# Points for discussion

1 What qualities of character did Muhammad show in his rise to power? Do you think he acted wisely in each difficulty he encountered?

2 What are the Five Pillars of the Faith? How important do you think they are? What rules would you lay down for the religious life?

3 What were the main difficulties that prevented a union between Jews, Muslims, and Christians during Muhammad's life? What have these three religions in common that could bring them closer together today?

4 Do you think that either the Kharijites or the Shi'ites were right in their attitude to the Caliph? Is there a place for wealth and power in the religious life?

5 In what ways do you consider the religion of Islam unsuited to our modern world? How should it be adapted to cope with the problems of the twentieth century?

# Sikhs, Jains, and Parsees

## 20. Notable minorities

In this chapter we shall study the beliefs of three communities which began as movements to reform the religious life of their day. Because they produced men and women of unusual strength of character, they have won widespread respect and influence, although in size they are quite small.

### Sikhs

The Sikhs are found mainly in the Punjab area of northern India and number about seven millions. The word *sikh* simply means 'disciple', and they are, in fact, disciples of Nanak, who lived from 1469 to 1538.

Nanak began life as a Hindu, but as he grew up he became increasingly dissatisfied with his religion. It is probable that as a young man he met another reformer, Kabir, who is always associated with the Sikh religion. Kabir declared that there was some truth in all religions but that there was only one God, though he was worshipped under many different names.

Nanak studied, in addition to Hinduism, the religion of Islam. Eventually, he left home and became a 'guru', or teacher. He travelled over India and Sri Lanka, and it is possible that he also visited Mecca, the holy city of Islam. He adopted a special dress which was partly Hindu and partly Muslim: the saffron-coloured robe of a Hindu holy man, and the turban and prayer beads of a Muslim. His object clearly was to bring together in one faith what he considered was the best in each religion and so effect a union between Hindus and Muslims.

He declared that there was one God, the creator of all

149

things, who should be loved and served. He was opposed to the Hindu caste system and he believed that women should be held in higher respect than they were under the old Hindu law of *Manu*. He advocated a temperate life without alcohol or tobacco. His followers should rise early in the day and take a cold bath before morning prayer.

Nanak was followed down the years by nine other gurus. The fifth guru, Arjan, built a most beautiful temple with golden domes on a small lake in the city of Amritsar. Though the Sikhs have many temples, this one is regarded as the centre of the Sikh religion. Every morning at sunrise the Sikh holy book, the *Adi Granth*, is placed in the temple, and throughout the day the scripture is chanted by a succession of readers. Worshippers enter the temple silently, bow with folded hands before it, and leave a gift before departing. Sikhs also eat together in their temples to show that there is no caste distinction amongst them.

The last Sikh guru, Gobind Singh, who died in 1708, taught that his followers should no longer expect a personal guru but that the teaching of the faith should henceforth be through the holy Scriptures (now Guru Granth) and the witness of the Sikh community (now Guru Panth or Khalsa). At fourteen years of age, boys and girls are accepted into the Khalsa in a solemn ceremony known as 'taking amrit' when hymns are sung, prayers offered and sweetened water is sprinkled on their heads and in their eyes.

Unfortunately, the Sikhs were badly persecuted by the Mogul Emperor in the seventeenth century, and thereupon they began to organize themselves into a fighting community. Each male Sikh took 'Singh', meaning 'lion', as an additional name and women took 'kaur', meaning 'princess'. At last they were able to hold their own against the Moguls, and in the eighteenth century, trained by French officers, they produced a first-class fighting force of 120,000. In the next century they fought the British in India, but were eventually defeated. Since then they have been close friends of the

British, supporting them in both world wars.

When the British left India in 1947, the Sikhs suffered terribly in the great waves of violence that spread over the country. Eventually, they were driven out of Pakistan. But they are a tough self-respecting race and quickly found new means of livelihood, though they have continually agitated for a separate state of their own. In search of a more peaceful existence, many have emigrated to the west.

Their violent history has earned for them a reputation as excellent fighting men. They vow always to do five things: to grow their hair long (hence their turbans) to wear a wooden comb, a steel bangle, shorts (often covered by trousers), and a small steel dagger.

They believe that their gurus were all perfect men and that through spiritual union with them they can find salvation. But the final goal is union with the supreme guru, God himself. When by self-denial and service to mankind this union is not achieved in one lifetime, they believe that re-incarnation becomes necessary.

## Jains

The Jains (pronounced Jines) are found in India. They take their name from a number of saints, jinas, of whom there are said to have been twenty-four in the history of the world. The first of these saints is reputed to have lived millions of years ago; the last of them, Mahavira, at about the same time as Gautama, the founder of Buddhism.

Mahavira was born of parents who were very religious; in fact, we are told that as a religious exercise they starved themselves to death. When Mahavira was thirty he became a holy man, pulling out all his hair and wandering through the country wearing a single garment. Later, he discarded even this. Like Gautama, he received enlightenment sitting under a tree. He became a jina, which means 'conqueror', having overcome evil, and then, like Gautama, he spent the rest of his life teaching and was very successful in making converts.

Buddhist writings confirm that he died in 476 B.C.

The teaching of the Jain religion is a mixture of Buddhism and Hinduism. The Jain scriptures take the place of the Hindu Vedas, though their priests are all brahmins. They do not accept the idea of a supreme God nor in theory do they really believe in the gods of Hinduism, yet Hindu gods are found in some of their temples. The temples are principally for the statues of their saints, whom they venerate above any god, because they have reached the perfect state.

This perfect state is the goal after which they all strive. Like the Hindu, they believe that the soul of each man continues to return to this world in bodily form until by meditation and good works it finally achieves liberation. In place, then, of a godhead there are separate souls who have reached the complete bliss of nirvana. Since reaching the state of nirvana means that one loses all contact henceforth with earthly life, it follows that in their temples Jains do not really worship before the great white statues of their saints, since they have all reached nirvana. The Jains must meditate upon their saints and thus hope to follow their good example.

Jains generally set a very fine example of the good life. They seek self-control in body and mind. They rise very early in the morning and go through a set ritual, repeating passages from the scriptures which they say again before retiring at night. They visit their temples frequently, offering gifts and making obeisance silently to the images of the saints. They are taught to be generous and kind to all living creatures and not on any account to take life. They are, of course, vegetarians. The Jain monk will take a broom with him to sweep away insects from his path, strain all the water he drinks, and even wears a cloth over his mouth to prevent the swallowing of insects. To all Jains violence in any form is wrong, and a criminal among them is rarely heard of. Because of their serious, well-disciplined lives they usually prosper in business and are generally found among the wealthier people in India.

## Parsees

Parsees are the followers of an ancient religion of Persia known as Zoroastrianism. They are found in India, mainly in Bombay, and they number just over one hundred thousand.

Zoroaster (the Greek name for the Persian Zarathrustra) lived in Persia between 630 and 553 B.C. His fellow-countrymen worshipped many gods similar to those in India. Zoroaster declared that there was only one god, the creator of all things. His name was Ahura Mazda, 'the Wise Lord'. There also existed, however, an evil spirit, Ahriman, who was perpetually at war with Ahura Mazda. This warfare accounted for the continuous struggle within the soul of man between good and evil. Sooner or later Ahura Mazda would be victorious, and Zoroaster hoped that he himself would live to witness the victory. The real purpose for which man was created was to assist Ahura Mazda to overcome the evil in the world. After death the human soul would have to pass over the Accountant's Bridge, where it would be decided according to his deeds whether he should go to heaven or to hell.

In the district of Media, where Zoroaster was born, there lived a number of scholarly men known as *magi*. They accepted his teaching and later were looked upon as the spiritual leaders of the religion. They produced the scriptures known as the *Avesta* and took care of the temples. As Zoroastrianism spread, some of the old Persian gods began to reappear, one of the chief being Mithra, whom the Romans worshipped as Mithras. In recent years the ruins of a temple to Mithras were found in the city of London.

In the seventeenth century A.D. the Muslims invaded Persia, and slowly Zoroastrianism had to give way to Islam. Many Persians left the country and most of them made their way to India, where they are known today as Parsees (Persians).

Their temples are known to us as 'Fire Temples', because within them a flame burns continuously as a symbol of the divine light that burns within the human soul. Parsees visit their temples frequently, removing their shoes as they enter and presenting gifts of sandalwood to the priests, who wear white robes and turbans. Non-Parsees are not allowed to enter.

They have many feast days. The last ten days of the year are specially reserved for charitable deeds. At the new year they wear new clothes, visit the temples, and then their friends, where they have a special ceremony in which they wish one another a happy new year.

Parsees are not allowed by their religion either to bury or burn their dead, for earth and fire are both considered sacred. Thus in India they have 'Towers of Silence', where the bodies of the dead are placed on stone slabs and the vultures allowed to eat the flesh. Later the bones slide down into a pit where they are consumed in lime. In smaller communities where there are no such towers burial is allowed, but lead coffins must be used.

The moral standards of Parsees are very high. Their aim in life is to be just, pure in mind and body, and of service to mankind. They have a great respect for education, believing that those who do not study are not serving God correctly. They are generally successful in business and consider that to tell a lie is the greatest evil.

# From Sikh, Jain, and Parsee Scriptures

May we be those who shall make life progressive and purposeful!

Assemble together, along with Justice, O Ahura Mazda and come hither

So that here where our thoughts formerly developed separately

They may now mature together, fuse and become widsom.

(Parsee prayer)

Some rules for Zoroastrian priests:

Avoid evil reputation.

Do not beat your teacher with a stick.

Whatever is taught to you deliver back to those who are worthy.

Rewards for the doers of good works and punishment for the workers of evil must be established by law, they are not to be administered by the clergy.

Keep ever progressing with the progress of this religion, do not go backwards.

Force malice away from your thoughts.

Obey the ruler and the priestly authority.

Those whose minds are at peace and who are free from passions do not desire to live at the expense of others.

(Jain scriptures)

As He was in the beginning the Truth,
So throughout the ages He has ever been the Truth
So even now He is Truth all-pervading
So for ever and ever he shall be Truth eternal.

(Sikh meditation)

# Points for discussion

1 Why do you think Nanak's attempt to unite Hindus and Muslims failed? What prevents people of different religions finding a means of worshipping together? Would it be a good thing to have one world religion?

2 Mahatma Gandhi found the religion of the Jains very helpful. From what you can find out about Gandhi, what part of their religion do you think attracted him most?

3 What features of the Parsee religion specially appeal to you?

# Humanism

## 21. People matter

Humanism, as its name suggests, has to do with human beings. When we say that someone is humane we mean that he is considerate, sympathetic, and kind to other people and to animals. The opposite of humane may be said to be inhuman: cruel, callous, and unfeeling. To be humanist in outlook, therefore, is to be very concerned about human beings, to regard man and his welfare as more important than anything else, more important today than money and power or even space-travel, and computers. 'People matter' would be a good humanist slogan because it means that in our very complex world, where all kinds of influences are felt and men are pursuing a thousand different aims, we must never lose sight of the fact that people matter most. The value of everything we do should therefore be tested by whether it will increase or diminish man's happiness in this world.

Great numbers of people are humanist in outlook in every generation, but there have been periods in history when life for the common man has been particularly grim and cheerless. At these times outstanding thinkers have tried to make their fellow-men feel again that the world should be run for the benefit of mankind. We shall consider three such periods and the way in which humanists reacted to them.

### The decline of Greece

About the year 308 B.C. a Greek philosopher and teacher, Epicurus, opened an academy or school for students just outside Athens. He taught them in a garden and consequently his followers were called 'the Garden Philosophers'.

Epicurus lived during one of the greatest revolutionary

periods in Greek history. You may have heard that the Greeks made experiments in a new form of government, democracy. They had been particularly proud of their city states, where every citizen had a vote and freedom to express his opinions. But in Epicurus's time Greece had become an imperial power. Alexander the Great had conquered the known world, and at his death his generals fought for what remained of his empire like jackals over a decaying carcass. In this turmoil free speech and the dignity of the individual citizen seemed to be disappearing for ever. Men were depressed and bewildered, and Epicurus offered them a way of life which he thought would help them.

In the first place, he declared that the world began as the result of a shower of atoms colliding with one another, and that further showers produced the universe. The gods lived somewhere in a remote region between the planets and took not the slightest interest in what happened to mankind. The universe and the world, therefore, were without any meaning or purpose. Men must accept the simple fact that the gods were no use to them, and they must help themselves. Epicurus believed that men's lives were governed by fear: fear of the gods and fear of death. The fear of the gods was meaningless because they had no contact with this world; the fear of death was unreasonable because nothing lay beyond it. 'When we are, death is not; when death is, we are not.' So death should mean nothing to us, because when our bodies died our souls died also.

He taught that the object of life should be pleasure, by which he really meant the absence of pain. To achieve this he thought that people should retire from the world. This would save them from worrying about politics and the state of their country. Then they should select those pleasures in life that would give them lasting satisfaction. This would not mean over-indulgence. Orgies of drinking or gambling, for instance, would inevitably end in misery. The original Epicureans in fact believed in living very simply. Over the gate of their celebrated garden they inscribed the warning that all who came there would be expected to live on barley cakes and water.

Epicurus fell ill of a painful disease, but he set a perfect example to his followers by bearing his sufferings patiently and without complaint until he died.

## The Renaissance

The Renaissance or New Learning came at the close of a bleak and harsh period in the life of the common man. During the Middle Ages, life in Europe had been run for the benefit of the ruling classes. The masses were poor and oppressed and considered of little value in the sight of God and man. Only the privileged few had either wealth or education.

Constantinople, far away in the East, was considered the centre of learning, and many famous scholars lived there. In 1453 it was sacked by the Muslims. Before this happened the scholars escaped and brought their books to Italy and other parts of Europe, where they became available to all who could read them. The invention of printing helped, and soon there was a tremendous urge for new learning to discover what great men in the past had said and believed. The leaders of the Christian Church frowned upon the spread of this kind of knowledge. They believed that they could do all the thinking about life that was necessary and then tell men what they should believe and how they should live. When, for instance, Tyndale translated the Bible into English, they tried to prevent its circulation and finally put him to death.

There were, however, a number of men who were determined that this new learning should spread. They are known as humanists because they believed that men were competent to judge for themselves what was good and true. They condemned the ignorance and superstition fostered by the Church and wanted men to find happiness and a full life on earth, not merely to hope for it in heaven.

Among them was a fine scholar, Erasmus. Though born in Rotterdam he lived most of his life in England. As a young man, persuaded by his family, he went into a monastery, but he hated the life so much that after seven years he came out and determined to attack one by one the abuses in the Church. He made fun of its superstitions and the political ambitions of the Pope. Although his criticisms were made in a humorous way, they were very severe, and he was feared and hated by monks and theologians. Though he remained in the Church, he would certainly have ended his days in the pitiless hands of the Inquisition, perhaps on the rack, had he not been protected by the King.

He condemned the violence and destruction of the times. 'It is the people,' he said, 'who build cities, while the madness of princes destroys them. Kings who are scarcely men are called "divine", "serene" though they turn the world upside down in a storm of war, "Catholic" though they follow anything rather than Christ.' And speaking of wars blessed by the Church, he declared that to use Christianity as a cloak for violence was to transform the dove of the Holy Spirit into a vulture.

With other humanists he encouraged the foundation of many grammar schools and revised the teaching in the universities. He translated the New Testament and urged men to put what they read there first in their lives. The simple and sincere Christian living that would result would restore to man the dignity he had lost.

*The Age of Revolution*

If you have read Charles Dickens' *A Tale of Two Cities* you will remember his vivid descriptions of the terrible hardships suffered by the French peasants. These were one cause of the Revolution in 1789. Conditions in many countries were similar. In England there was great poverty and unemployment, provoking the Luddite riots and eventually the Chartist movement. Many people were appalled by the conditions of the working classes in every country, and agitated for reform and new ideals in government that would produce better social conditions.

Jeremy Bentham was one of these reformers. As a boy he was brilliant; he was nicknamed 'the Professor' at school and took his degree at Oxford University when he was only fifteen years of age. He sacrificed a legal career in order to work for reform. Having a thorough knowledge of the law, he made a detailed study of the punishment of crime and advocated more humane ways of dealing with criminals. He pressed for reforms which we have now long enjoyed: universal suffrage, annual parliaments, paid representatives, and vote by ballot. He declared that the object of government should be the greatest happiness of the greatest number. His books were translated into French and had great influence abroad. When he died, out of respect for his wishes, his body was dissected, and his skeleton, dressed in his usual robes, presented to University College, London, where it is still to be seen.

A Frenchman, Auguste Comte, was a well-known member of a group of philosophers who discussed in a more general way how men should live. He believed that philosophy should be concerned with man, not God. Man was the centre of the universe and his problems could be solved by sociology (a word he coined) and by science, which would take the place of religion. It was Man who should be worshipped. He devised a church and a priesthood, and two of his friends actually founded a church in England for the worship of Man.

A famous man who was influenced by both Bentham and Comte was John Stuart Mill. He had a brilliant mind. We are told that he was learning Greek at the age of three. He believed that liberty was the most important aim in life, and that every man should have freedom to develop his own personality. Happiness was essential, but it could best be obtained by pursuing other aims such as helping people or being absorbed in one's job.

These three men, typical of many like them, were convinced that something was radically wrong with the way men lived in this world. They offered new ideals and new methods of attaining them.

## Modern humanism

You will notice that the Epicureans were concerned with the individual rather than the state, whereas Bentham was concerned more with the state and how it was governed. Modern humanism combines both these attitudes.

We must find happiness for ourselves by making the best of our lives, using our bodies and minds to their fullest extent. We should be interested in everything, ready for new ideas and new adventures, and not content merely to sit about and watch what other people do, as, for example, on TV. We live in a marvellous world and a wonderful age, and the few years we have on this planet should be enjoyed to the full.

On the other hand, humanists are deeply concerned about their fellow-men. They direct us to examine 'The Universal Declaration of Human Rights' issued by the United Nations in 1948. Here it states that men are born free, equal in rights and dignity. Everyone should remain free and have equal protection before the law. They should have freedom of thought, conscience, speech, and religion, choice of employment, favourable working conditions, just pay, and a standard of living adequate for the health and well-being of themselves and their dependants. Yet nearly half the human race today is underfed, millions endure shocking living conditions, and thousands suffer persecution, wrongful imprisonment, and even death. Humanists will therefore take a keen interest in government both national and international, and in all social service, because for them above everything else 'people matter'.

How is this attitude to life related to religion? This opens a wide field for discussion. Some people assure us that it is their religion that gives them a deep concern for their fellow-men. Gautama, the founder of Buddhism, was impelled by his pity for mankind to sacrifice nirvana and spend his life teaching Buddhism.

Confucius, whose sole concern was the salvation of China, asserted that Heaven had sent him and that Heaven protected him. Christians in all ages have devoted their lives to good works as a result, they declare, of direct inspiration from God. In the nineteenth century, Shaftesbury's concern for children and Wilberforce's concern for slaves, and in this century, Mother Teresa's concern for the poor in India, are outstanding examples. Dr. Kaunda of Zambia, speaking about Christian humanism in Africa, said, 'the most important factor in life is man whom Christ came to serve'.

Nevertheless, modern humanism as represented in Britain, for example by the British Humanist Association and the National Secular Society, is opposed to religion. Their members do not believe in the existence of God because this involves an act of faith which they assert is a betrayal of reason. They feel, too, that religion has proved a hindrance rather than a help in the battle for reform. And it is true, as we have seen, that on occasion the Christian church has impeded the advance of knowledge and blocked the path of reform. In any case they maintain that in this scientific age religion is no longer necessary; man, not God, should now take the centre of the stage. Thus, on behalf of humanity, they campaign persistently for individual freedom, international peace and the relief of world poverty.

But whatever may be the source of our inspiration, the really important concern of humanists is that we should live full, free and useful lives with a keen eye for the welfare of our fellow human beings. 'This is the true joy in life,' said Bernard Shaw, 'the being used for a purpose recognised by yourself as a mighty one; the being thoroughly worn out before you are thrown on the scrapheap; the being a force of Nature instead of a feverish little clod of ailments and grievances complaining that the world will not devote itself to making you happy.'

# Points for discussion

1 What are the main problems that mankind is facing today? What is being done to solve them? What else do you think should be done?

2 The poet Swinburne wrote:

> 'Glory to man in the highest!
> For man is the master of things.'

Modern humanism maintains that man, in this scientific age, has no further need of belief in God. Do you agree?

3 Find out what you can about Charles Darwin and Bertrand Russell. What contribution would you say they made towards human progress?

# Communism

## 22. The theory of Communism

The word 'Communism' owes its importance today to the work and teaching of Karl Marx, who died in 1883. Before Marx it had been used by idealists to describe a state of society where everyone would enjoy a fair share of the total wealth that its members produced. One or two attempts had been made to found such a society. Possibly the most notable one was that of the first converts to Christianity. We find a reference to it in the Bible: 'All whose faith had drawn them together held everything in common. They would sell their property and possessions and make a general distribution as the need of each required' (Acts 2:44, 45). A world so fashioned would certainly have been a very wonderful place in which to live. Unfortunately, the experiment failed. The reason for its failure can be gathered from the writings of later Christian leaders, who suggest that for such an experiment to succeed, man must love God and his neighbour with very deep sincerity. Apparently, the early Christians did not measure up to these requirements.

The twentieth-century experiment has also failed. The main objective of the Communist Revolution has never been reached, and a communist state of society does not exist, either in Russia, China, or anywhere else. This will become clear as we study the work of Karl Marx.

### Karl Marx

Karl Marx was born in 1818 in the Rhineland. He was a Jew. His original name was Levi and his father was descended from a long line of Jewish rabbis. Soon after Karl's birth, however, his father was converted to the Christian faith, and with his family was baptized, Karl being brought up as a member of the Lutheran Church.

As a young man on the Continent Marx soon became aware of the terrible poverty suffered by the working classes as a result of the Industrial Revolution. He was appalled by the squalid state in which men, women, and children lived, forced to work long hours, often in unhealthy and brutalizing conditions, while a small section of the community, the capitalists, grew rich at their expense. In Germany, as a consequence, there was a general atmosphere of unrest, secret working-men's societies were formed, and Marx felt this to be the most urgent problem of his lifetime.

He was sent to Bonn and Berlin Universities to study law. But already he was becoming something of an agitator, and because of his views he was soon in trouble with the authorities and had to give up his career. This was a great blow to his father, who was a lawyer himself. For Marx, however, this was only a first step in his renunciation of his past life. He became anti-Jewish and never referred to himself again as a Jew or wished to admit his Jewish origin. He also rejected Christianity and became an atheist – one who denies the existence of God.

Marx was now thrown upon his own resources. He turned to journalism to make a little money; he read widely, especially philosophy, economics, and politics; and in 1843 he went to live in Paris, where there were many other political exiles. He also spent some time in Brussels, where he met Friedrich Engels, who remained his friend and fellow-worker for the rest of his life. Engels was a German philosopher converted to Communism. He was also a well-to-do businessman in charge for some years of a branch of his father's business in Manchester. He read and wrote much on the subject of Communism, supplied Marx with information on business practice and, above all, supplied him regularly with money. Marx and Engels founded the German Workers' Society.

They were greatly encouraged in their efforts by the widespread unrest in Germany and Austria. In 1847, at an International Congress of Workers held in London, the Communist League was formed, and in 1848 Marx and Engels issued their famous Communist Manifesto. This called upon the workers of the world to unite; they had nothing to lose but their chains! Unfortunately for Marx, the revolutions that broke out in Germany and Austria in 1848 collapsed. Many members of the Communist League were arrested and suffered harsh sentences, and later the League was disbanded.

Marx found refuge in London. He intended to remain there only a short time. In fact, he spent the remainder of his life in England, and much of it in the Reading Room of the British Museum. He enlarged the Communist Manifesto into a series of books on the theory of communism, the most important of which is entitled *Das Kapital*. These works became the Bible of the communist movement. But Marx himself saw little practical result from his labours. In 1864 he helped to found 'the First International' (the International Working Men's Association), but this later dissolved because he quarrelled with those in the organization who challenged his views.

Marx's teaching provoked probably the most ruthless and terrifying revolutions the world has ever seen. Yet Marx's nature showed no streak of violence. It is true that he was domineering and sometimes ill-tempered, but he was a law-abiding citizen, happily married to a Scotswoman of aristocratic birth, and very fond of his children. He had a first-class brain and was a tremendous worker, but he suffered from ill health and for most of his life had to endure the humiliations of poverty. Moreover, he died a disappointed man, long before his ideas were put into action, for the Russian Revolution did not take place until 1917.

Few people have read all that Marx wrote. His books are long and difficult to understand, and his followers have

167

continually argued and quarrelled about their meaning. The following summary, dealing with his interpretation of history and economics, should help us to grasp the basic ideas of his teaching.

## The materialist conception of history

Marx studied the development of mankind from primitive times. He was particularly interested in the way men lived together and how they organised society. Over many thousands of years this organisation revealed a pattern of change which Marx felt to be very important. Here briefly are his conclusions. If we could pierce the mists of antiquity we should find that the earliest men lived in a communist society. But as the population increased this was superseded by a slave-owning system such as the great civilisations of Egypt, Greece, and Rome produced. Eventually, the slave-owning society disappeared and the feudal system emerged. But as money gradually replaced barter, so capitalism replaced the feudal system. Now, argued Marx, the era of capitalism is at last drawing to a close and the communist system is about to take its place.

Marx declared that this process in history was inevitable: it was governed by certain laws and nothing could alter it. Thus communism was bound to overthrow capitalism, and it would be useless to resist it.

Marx had no doubt that he was right because he was convinced that he had discovered the laws that governed these changes in society. He was an atheist and a materialist and for him the only things in life that were real were those which men could see and handle. God, for instance, did not exist, so he could have no influence on man's destiny. Human relationships were of little account. The loves and hates of people in power or the passions that stirred men's hearts, such as patriotism and race prejudice, were unimportant. For Marx only one fact seemed vital. No matter how gifted or well educated a man might be, he could not live unless he had

168

food. It was therefore the economic system, the struggle for food and shelter, and later for all the goods and services that men produced, that decided the course of history. Art, literature, music, religion, all that men thought and believed, these were merely the result of the economic system under which they happened to be living.

These systems changed because none of them was perfect. Each had its own weaknesses, and over the years an opposition mounted until it was stronger than the system itself, and overthrew it. Then a new system appeared more in keeping with the needs of the time. But perhaps what interests us most at this point is how Marx knew that one of these great revolutionary changes was about to take place and why it should result in universal communism. To understand this we must consider his interpretation of the economic theory of surplus value.

*The theory of surplus value*

Under the capitalism system, according to Marx, there exist two classes permanently in opposition to each other, the capitalists and the workers. The capitalists own the means of production, the factories, materials, and machinery; the workers own nothing, and have only their labour to sell to the highest bidder.

Now the real value of anything the capitalist produces is the value of the labour required to make it. For example, let us suppose that the total labour cost required to produce and sell a certain motor-car is £4,000. This is its real value. If it is sold for £5,000, the difference, £1,000, is its surplus value. A thousand such cars will sell for £5 million, but the workers will receive only £4 million. Two results of this system now become clear. The capitalist pockets the surplus value and the workers do not receive sufficient wages to buy back the goods they have manufactured. In fact, out of these thousand cars the capitalist will have two hundred left on his hands, if he depends solely on the workers as his customers. He must therefore find markets elsewhere. For this reason, Marx declared, capitalist countries are continually competing with one another for markets abroad, and thus annexing new territories and building empires. But there must be a limit to available markets, and in due course this relentless struggle issues in nations fighting one another and the system collapsing.

At the same time as this fatal competition is proceeding, the workers are becoming poorer and more numerous, while the capitalists are becoming richer and fewer in number as they combine to form larger firms. This opposition of capitalists and workers is known as the class war. In their increasing misery the workers will draw closer together, and when the system begins to crack, they will drive out the capitalists, seize the means of production, and take over the government of the state.

Marx thought that the poverty and political unrest he saw around him in Europe was an unmistakable sign that the revolution was about to take place.

After the revolution there will come the second stage in the achievement of communism – the socialist phase. This will be a period of some years in which the workers' leaders, having seized power, will clear the country of capitalists and build up sufficient forces to resist any attempt to reinstate them. During this period, government is bound to be autocratic and sometimes harsh.

Finally, the third stage – the era of true communism – will appear. All opponents of the revolution having been liquidated, there will emerge a classless society, one of complete equality and justice. Government will no longer be necessary and will wither away. The maintenance of order, the production and distribution of wealth, the care of all citizens will be arranged by friendly agreements between the workers. The guiding principle of this ideal society will be: 'From each according to his ability, to each according to his need.'

# Communism

## 23. Communism in action

We must now consider the various ways in which men have tried to put the teaching of Karl Marx into practice. But before doing so it is necessary to refer briefly to the general movement for reform in the nineteenth century, and to see how Marx's ideas fitted into it.

*Socialism*

Many people besides Marx were distressed by the shocking social conditions arising from the Industrial Revolution. They were tremendously active; writing, arguing, forming societies, issuing newspapers and pamphlets, addressing large public meetings, all with the object of bringing about the urgent reforms they felt necessary. Their ideas varied considerably, but on one important point most of them agreed: that industry must no longer remain in private hands for the benefit of the few, but must be brought under public control for the benefit of everyone. Those who accepted this principle were known as Socialists.

They disagreed on the nature of public ownership. Some believed that the state should be the owner and that Parliament should control industry. Others argued that Parliament and the Civil Service, which carries out its wishes, were too remote to keep in touch with the requirements of each industry. Smaller groups, such as the trades unions, would be more efficient. It was essential that the workers themselves should have a large measure of control.

There was also serious disagreement as to how the change from private to public ownership should be effected. On this matter Socialists divided into two main parties: Evolutionists and Revolutionists.

The Evolutionists believed that the change could be successfully achieved by Acts of Parliament. Parliament should interfere in the running of industry, by laying down conditions and hours of work, and establishing a national minimum wage. Gradually public opinion would be educated until it demanded complete state ownership. This nationalisation of industry would be first applied to key industries, such as railways, gas, electricity, and coal-mining, and having proved its worth, would go on and embrace the rest.

Marx, as the champion of the Revolutionary Socialists, dismissed Evolutionary Socialism as Utopian, based on woolly minded idealism. He argued that governments were merely the lackeys of the capitalists, who would fight in the last resort to retain their property. Gradual improvements in the lot of the worker would take generations. Meanwhile the masses were already desperate and would continue to sink into greater depths of misery and despair. This forecast did not prove correct in the case of his adopted country, Britain. It was, however, true of the one country where his theories were first tried out.

*Russia*

Marx hated Russia. He was a German and inherited the deep-seated hostility that the two countries felt for each other. Moreover, he could never have imagined Russia as the centre of the first Communist Revolution. Eighty per cent of her population worked on the land, and his theories about revolution applied to workers in industry, not to peasants.

Nevertheless, in 1917 Russia was on the brink of revolution, communist or otherwise. For centuries it had been a very backward country. Seventy years after the French Revolution the masses in Russia were still serfs, bought and sold with the land on which they lived. Only in 1861 were they freed, and then into conditions that made many of them worse off than under serfdom. There was continual unrest throughout the country.

The trouble lay with the government. The Russian kings were known as Tsars, and they ruled as dictators. Occasionally they would make some little effort to improve the lot of the ignorant and downtrodden peasants, but often, at the first sign of dissatisfaction with their inadequate reforms, they would become frightened and no further progress would be made for years. Some of the Tsars were kindly men by nature, but they could not imagine their country changing. They believed that their subjects liked to be told what to do and to be punished when they disobeyed. Even in 1917, when the country was in turmoil, Nicholas II, the last Tsar, who with his family was murdered by the communists, acted on the principle, 'Russia likes to feel the whip'. He ordered his troops to fire on the rebellious crowds until they refused to fire any more and, in fact, joined the revolutionaries themselves.

During the latter part of the nineteenth century much of the opposition to the Russian tyranny was organized by university students. They attempted on a number of occasions to assassinate the Tsar or one of his ministers. Usually their efforts failed, but in 1881 they succeeded in killing Alexander II by throwing a bomb under his carriage. Six years later a young man from a small town on the banks of the Volga was one of a group executed for attempting to kill Alexander's successor. It was a commonplace event, except for one fact: the young man happened to be the brother of Vladimir Ilyich Ulyanov, who later took the name of Lenin.

## Lenin

Lenin was born in 1870 of a middle-class family and was trained in the law. His brother's execution filled him with hatred for the Russian tyranny and for thirty years he worked tirelessly to overthrow it. He suffered imprisonment, and exile in Siberia, but for most of the time he was in hiding abroad.

Lenin was converted to communism by reading Marx, and he wished to see a communist revolution in Russia. During his exile he gave this much thought, his main problem being how to apply Marxism to an agricultural country. The peasants he regarded as lower middle class and there were relatively few workers in industry. At first he thought that the only possible revolution would be one initiated by the middle classes, with his workers' party joining in the government that they would establish. Then he changed his mind. He would secretly form and train in Russia a professional revolutionary party. If at some time general unrest broke out, he could then use it as a spearhead movement to establish a communist dictatorship.

His opportunity came during the First World War. In 1917 the German armies were slowly destroying Russia. They realised the turmoil that existed behind the Russian lines and someone had the brilliant idea that if they could smuggle the exiled Lenin into Russia, he would make it worse. So they offered him and his fellow-revolutionaries a sealed train from Switzerland to the Baltic coast. He instantly accepted the offer and reached Leningrad via Sweden on 16 April 1917. His genius immediately showed itself. Within seven months and with scarcely a shot fired on his behalf, he quietly established himself as dictator of Russia.

The next few years were a nightmare for him. He had immediately to find armies to fight the White Russians (the opponents of the Revolution) and also the British, French, Japanese, Czechoslovakians, and Americans, all of whom sent troops to overthrow the regime because they felt it dangerous to the peace of Europe. In the end he beat them all. But his troubles were not over. The normal life of the country was in chaos as food supplies had failed and the workers' control of industry proved a complete failure. In desperation, Lenin had to reintroduce a modified form of capitalism known as the New Economic Policy.

As a dictator, Lenin was quite ruthless, instituting a reign of terror against his enemies. In his own mind his actions were justified, because he believed that communist revolutions were about to break out all over Europe, and the period of dictatorship would soon be over. When they failed to do so, he found an explanation for it. He declared that the capitalists still had many backward people to exploit and only when this process was exhausted would the universal class war take place. For communists this remains the official explanation of the continued survival of capitalism, and it is a very effective part of their ceaseless propaganda in backward countries.

## Marx–Leninism

Lenin died in 1924. He left Russia poor, but he had achieved his main ambition: to carry through the Revolution and to establish a form of government which would lead, he imagined, to the true state of communism Marx had dreamed of.

Very little advance has been made in this direction since. Though, since Lenin, we have seen communism established in many smaller states in Europe and also in China, the pattern of government remains very similar to that which exists in Russia. It is Lenin's adaptation of Marx and may be called for convenience Marx–Leninism.

It is very far from Marx's ideals, but then Marx's elaborate prophecies did not come true. There has been no Marxian class war anywhere. Communism has been established in one country after another, not by a popular working-class rising but by a relatively small, highly organised group of revolutionaries known as the Communist Party. It is this minority party and not the workers that rules communist countries. In Russia, for example, only about one person in twenty belongs to the Party, and it is Party members alone whom the Russian people are allowed to elect as their rulers.

It soon became obvious that the Russian revolution was not going to be followed by mass working-class revolutions in other countries. So Stalin, Lenin's successor, decided that his best policy would be to make Russia a great power. This he did by building huge industries and making the peasants work on state-owned farms known as Collectives. He annexed the territory of other countries, half Poland and the Baltic States, and imposed communism by means of the Russian Army on Hungary, Rumania, Czechoslovakia, Albania, Bulgaria, and East Germany, now known with Russia as the Communist Bloc. All this entailed enormous suffering. It is believed that Stalin's ruthless policy caused the death of about ten million people in Russia alone, apart from other countries. But when he died Russia was one of the greatest military and economic powers in the world.

Communists have talked a great deal about 'liberating' the workers of other countries, which means military action to overthrow their governments, and this threat has made both Russia and China greatly feared by other nations. Where this liberation took place, as in the case of Russia's satellite states, Russia retained complete control over the liberated people for many years. They were compelled to adopt the Party line from Moscow without question. The grim alternative was re-invasion, such as Hungary and Czechoslovakia suffered. But recently some changes have been taking place. The satellite states appear to be slowly gaining a measure of political independence. In industry, too, a new freedom is emerging. Instead of all directives coming from Moscow, greater responsibility is being given to local officials both to find markets and to offer workers cash incentives for more and better work.

Marx believed that art and literature reflected the economic life of the people; the communists insist that they must. From birth children are indoctrinated with communist principles, and what they read and learn is most carefully supervised. The literature of other countries has been selected so as to portray the worst aspects of capitalist society. But here again there are signs of change. The educational straitjacket is not fitting quite so well as it used to do. People are thinking more for themselves, meeting more foreigners, reading more widely, and wishing to express themselves with greater freedom. As a consequence, many fine men and women who refuse to toe the Party Line are found in prison or in 'remedial hospitals'.

Again, in religion the demand for freedom persists. The government has provided intensive anti-religious education for fifty years and has always discriminated against people who practised their faith, especially the Jews. Yet religion survives.

All this goes to show that men value personal freedom very highly. It does not prove that communism is a failure. Far from it. In Russia it has shown remarkable growth and stability. Before the Revolution her people were poor, ignorant, and constantly in danger of death from violence or starvation. All this has disappeared. Every child is educated and every adult is assured of security. Social services are free, pensions are available, and housing provided. Apart from Party élite who enjoy special privileges, the worker is paid according to his skill or responsibility, and there is nothing to prevent him from becoming well-to-do and leaving his money to his children. In fact, in a scientific and technological age Russia has become one of the foremost countries in the world.

China became a People's Republic in 1949. Mao-Tze-tung, after assisting in the defeat of the Japanese and later defeating the Nationalist army of Chiang Kai-shek, became its first Chairman. For twenty-seven years he presided over the country with increasing power, and the little Red Book, *The Thoughts of Chairman Mao*, became virtually China's bible. He was one of the ablest rulers the world has seen and under his guidance China made immense strides, socially and economically. He was greatly assisted in this by Chou-En-lai who held the premiership for thirty years.

Mao concentrated first on agriculture and the vast peasant

population in whose loyalty he had great faith. With very little bloodshed the reigning landlords were relieved of their holdings and gradually huge communes were created and controlled by peasant committees. In industry likewise the management was transferred to workers' revolutionary committees. Later Mao realized that the system was creating a new élite, an upper class of bosses and bureaucrats, so in 1966 he launched the Cultural Revolution.

Millions of young people, called Red Guards, were allowed to roam the country exposing class enemies, mainly intellectuals, known as 'capitalist roadsters'. Party officials, work bosses, lecturers and teachers suffered violence and humiliation. Many thousands died in their distress and throughout the country order was giving place to chaos. The Revolution was called off in 1968. The good results, however, were a simplifying of central administration and a more democratic relationship between bosses and workers. To maintain this sense of equality it was decreed that all intellectuals in future should spend some time working on the land.

Great advances were made in education and health. In 1949 85 per cent of the population was illiterate; as early as 1967 illiteracy had all but disappeared among those under forty. In medicine, for example, infant mortality of 140 per thousand in 1949 had dropped to 21 in 1970. But this resulted in an alarming increase in population: 540,000,000 in 1949 became over 1,000,000,000 in the 1980s. Faced with this problem, the government declared that men should not marry before the age of twenty-two and women, twenty. Also considerable benefits would be granted to families who restricted themselves to one child.

Mao realized that China's long standing policy of isolation was a disadvantage and in the 1970s diplomatic relations and trade treaties were effected with other countries including Japan and the U.S.A. Relations with Russia, however, remained hostile for many reasons including ideological disagreement and border disputes.

After Mao's death, the government was faced with the problem of declining production. The workers seemed to lack enthusiasm. As a last resort, as in Russia, a measure of free enterprise was introduced. Industry was granted more independence and the workers new incentives; in agriculture, workers, once they had met the state quota, were allowed to sell surplus produce on a free market for private profit. This resulted in a great increase in production.

Mao for some time was much in favour of criticism of the regime and young people expressed candid views which in Russia would certainly have earned them a prison sentence if nothing worse. More recently this freedom has been limited but religion, for example, is tolerated without persecution. Nevertheless, as tourists discover, China remains a police state, free association with foreigners is frowned upon, and anyone who declares himself opposed to communist rule is not tolerated.

Both Russia and China have achieved material progress hitherto unknown in human history. To have raised more than a quarter of the world's entire population out of poverty, illiteracy and ill health in comparatively few years is little short of a miracle. It has demanded faith and dedication on a vast scale. Yet it has also involved severe loss of personal liberty, considerable suffering and, especially in Russia, an appalling sacrifice of human life.

Moreover, the ideal state, as Marx imagined it, has never emerged. No communist government has shown any tendency to wither away. But Marx's hatred of poverty and injustice still poses the question: can we devise a political system that combines personal freedom with social equality and economic security?

# Points for discussion

1 Do you consider Marx's interpretation of history a sufficient explanation of man's progress?

2 Why have Marx's prophecies about the class war not been realized?

3 What do you think is the best form of control for industry? How can it be achieved?

4 Propaganda is one of the most powerful weapons today. What can we learn from the way the communists and capitalists use it?

5 'From each according to his ability, to each according to his need.' Is communism possible? How can it be achieved?

# Index

# Index

# INDEX

Stalin, 176
*Sudras*, 19
Sufism, 143, 144
Sukkot, Feast of Tabernacles, 93
Sunnis, 143
surplus value, theory of, 169
Swinburne, poet, 164
sympathetic magic, 2
synagogue, 88, 90, 91 fol., 96

### T

taboo, 2
Tacitus, historian, 103
*Tale of Two Cities*, 160
*Talmud*, Jewish, 87 fol., 99
TAOISM
    Chuang Tzu, 69
    Lao-tze, 67
    mysticism, 69
    *Tao*, the, 68 fol.
    *Yin-yang*, 70
*Tao-te-ching, The Book of the Way*,
    68
temples
    fire, 153–4
    Hindu, 12
Ten Commandments, 36, 83, 88
Teresa, Mother, 163
theosophy, 21
Theravada Buddhism, 42, 47
Tibet, 44, 46, 48
Titus, general, 81
*Torah*, 87 fol., 92, 95, 96, 97, 99
*torii*, 71
totem, 4
Towers of Silence, 154
Turkey
    centre of Muslim world, 141–2
    invasion of, 141
    modern, 145
Tyndale, reformer, 159
Tsars, Russian, 173

### U

Ulamas, 144
Ulyanov, Vladimir Ilyich, 173 fol.
Universal Declaration of Human
    Rights, 162
universe, origin of, 158
untouchables, 20, 24
*Upanishads*, scriptures, 10, 15 fol.
Ur, 82
usury, 86, 137

### V

*Vaisyas*, 19
Varuna, god, 9
*Vedas*, scriptures, 10
Vehicles, larger and lesser, 42 fol.
Vishnu, god, 8, 9, 10, 11, 18

### W

Wahhabis sect, 143
Way, the People of the, 117
'Way of the Gods, the,' 71
Wesley, John, 122
Wilberforce, 163
Williams, John, missionary, 123
witchdoctor, 2, 3
women
    Buddha's attitude to, 39
    Hindu attitude to, 25 fol.
    Muslim attitude to, 138
World Council of Churches, 124

### Y

Yahweh, 82
*yin-yang*, 70
yoga, 17–18, 33, 34
Yom Kippur, Day of Atonement,
    93

### Z

Zealots, 105
Zen-Buddhism, 43–4
Zoroastrianism, 153
Zulus, 1, 5

exchanged and apples dipped in honey are eaten.

The Day of Atonement (Yom Kippur), is the last day of ten days' penitence following the New Year. It is a day of prayer, confession and repentance. A devout Jew may fast for 24 hours and spend most of his time in the synagogue. The day recalls the one occasion in the year when the High Priest used to enter the Holy of Holies and also make prayer and sacrifice for the people.

The Feast of Tabernacles (Sukkot) follows five days later. It is a reminder of God's care for the Israelites in the wilderness of Sinai. The synagogue is decorated with fruit and flowers; shelters (tabernacles) made of branches are erected in gardens or near the synagogue and meals taken there during the following week.

The Festival of Lights (Hannukah) is a joyful occasion about the time of Christmas in the Christian calendar. It is in memory of the great victory of Judas Maccabeus and the rededication of the Temple in 164 B.C.E. The festival lasts eight days and each day a fresh candle is lit, children receive presents and games are often played.

The Passover or the Feast of Unleavened Bread (Pesach) takes place around the time of the Christian Easter. At home on the eve of the Passover, the youngest child asks the question 'Why is this night different from all other nights?' Then his father explains how it recalls a night 3,000 years ago when their ancestors were slaves in Egypt and during the hours of darkness the Angel of Death smote the Egyptians and Moses led the Israelites out into the desert. During the Passover meal (Seder) and for the next eight days the family eats Matzos, unleavened bread, reminding them of the exodus, and a nut and apple paste to remind them of the mortar which they used to make bricks for the Egyptians.

Pentecost or the Feast of Weeks (Shavuot) follows fifty days of mourning after Passover. It recalls the failure of the Jewish revolt against Rome in the second century and it also commemorates Moses receiving the Law from God. The announced that the first five books of the Old Testament were not written by Moses at all, but centuries after he had died. Today we know that some of this early criticism was extreme and ill-considered, but few people realised this at the time. The results were serious: many Jews lost their faith altogether; others clung to their belief in God and his special providence for the Jewish race, while they began to give up the religious customs and traditions based on the *Torah*.

## The effect of assimilation on Judaism

Meanwhile Jewish communities everywhere were learning to live in harmony with the Gentile nations. They felt that they must prove their loyalty to their adopted countries by conforming to their way of life. Remarkable changes occurred. Many Jews refused to consider themselves any longer as a separate nation: they were merely a sect with certain religious beliefs. Synagogue services were altered to conform with the pattern of Christian worship. Hebrew gave place to the language of the country; Sunday was adopted as the day of rest instead of Saturday; men and women sat together in the synagogue; their children were 'confirmed' at Whitsuntide.

On the other hand, many Jews were scandalized by these 'modernist' tendencies. The only hope for the race, they felt, was to turn a deaf ear to all modern criticism and maintain rigidly the ancient customs and beliefs of their faith. Such people today are known as Orthodox Jews. They accept the *Torah*, which should be studied daily, as the supreme authority. Its laws especially in relation to the sabbath and to diet should be rigidly observed. Prayers should be said three times a day; children given regular instruction in the faith; and the local rabbi treated with the highest respect. Orthodox Jews would not accept women as rabbis. They believe that Messiah will come to restore Israel to her rightful place among the nations and eventually draw all men unto him.

As might be expected, a middle party eventually arose. They stood firm for the Jewish way of life and kept an open